EUROPEAN CONSTITUTIONALISM

HISTORICAL AND CONTEMPORARY PERSPECTIVES

P.I.E. Peter Lang

Bruxelles · Bern · Berlin · Frankfurt am Main · New York · Oxford · Wien

EUROCLIO is a scientific and editorial project, a network of research institutions and researchers, and an ideas forum. EUROCLIO as an editorial project consists of two aspects: the first concerns studies and documents, the second concerns tools. Both are aimed at making the results of research more accessible, and also at opening up paths through the history of European construction/integration/unification.

The EUROCLIO series meets a dual objective:

- to provide reference tools for research,
- to provide a platform for this research in terms of the publication of results.

The series thus consists of two sub-series that satisfy these requirements: the Studies and Documents series and the References series. These two series are aimed at general libraries and/or university history departments, teachers and researchers, and in certain cases, specific professional circles.

The Studies and Documents series consists of monographs, collections of articles, conference proceedings, and collections of texts with notes for teaching purposes.

The References series consists of bibliographies, guides and other tools. It thus contributes to the creation of a database making up a "Permanent catalogue of sources and bibliographies on European construction".

Edited by
Éric Bussière, Université de Paris-Sorbonne (France),
Michel Dumoulin, Louvain-la-Neuve (Belgique),
& Antonio Varsori, Universitá degli Studi di Padova (Italia)

EUROPEAN CONSTITUTIONALISM

HISTORICAL AND CONTEMPORARY PERSPECTIVES

Alexandre DUPEYRIX & Gérard RAULET (eds.)

Euroclio
No. 83

The editors would like to thank their research group UMR 8138 IRICE, the Excellence Cluster Labex EHNE ("Ecrire une Nouvelle Histoire de l'Europe") and the Doctoral School "Civilisa-tions, Cultures, Littératures et Sociétés" of the University Paris-Sorbonne for their intellectual and financial support.

This publication has been peer-reviewed.

Éditions scientifiques internationales
Brussels, 2014
1 avenue Maurice, B-1050 Brussels, Belgium
pie@peterlang.com ; www.peterlang.com

ISSN 0944-2294
ISBN 978-2-87574-192-9 (paperback)
ISBN 978-3-0352-6454-8 (eBook)
D/2014/5678/67

CIP available from the British Library, UK and from the Library of Congress, USA.

"Die Deutsche National Bibliothek" lists this publication in the "Deutsche Nationalbibliografie"; detailed bibliographic data is available on the Internet at <http://dnb.de>.

Contents

Introduction

Alexandre Dupeyrix & Gérard Raulet

The deep economic crisis Europe has been facing for several years can be seen as both a cause and a consequence of the political indecision in which the European Community/Union has been living for so long now. The end-goal (the *finalité*) of this unique political project has never been clarified. While its objective – to guarantee peace, security, justice and wealth – was certainly explicit from the start and has been repeated in the various treaties founding the Community or Union, the institutional and political means necessary to attain these goals have so far remained undetermined. In these times of turmoil, this indetermination turns out to be the latent defect of the European Union.

If truth be told, the European project has always been caught in a series of paradoxes or antinomies that seem to be inherent to it. How, for example, can we build a political entity if the political subject is not yet identified, if there is no such thing as a 'European people'? How can we have a people of citizens without a political constitution? And how can we have a political constitution without a European people? These antinomies probably have something to do with the teleological nature of the European project. European integration is a process the end of which is not defined in advance. The founding fathers of the European community were well aware of the processual and regulative dimension of the European idea, and they were at the very least unclear about the institutional form the European Community should take. Jean Monnet looking back in the 1970s at the first decades of the European construction wrote in his *Memoirs* (1976):

> I could not say where necessity will take us, what kind of Europe awaits us, for it is impossible to imagine today the decisions that may be taken in tomorrow's context. The most important thing is to hold on to the few fixed points that have guided us from day one: to create, gradually, between the men and women of Europe the widest common interest possible, managed by common democratic institutions to which sufficient sovereignty is delegated. This dynamic is still at work today. […] I have never doubted that this process would lead us one day to the United States of Europe, but I do not try to imagine today the political framework we will adopt, so imprecise are

> the terms we argue about: confederation, federation. What we are preparing, through the action of the European Community, is unprecedented. This community is itself based on institutions that will have to be reinforced, but the true political authority European democracies will one day designate has yet to be conceived of and realised.[1]

It seems that this task ("conceiving a real political authority") is still ahead of us. Remaining very vague about a possible deadline and the circumstances under which this goal might be achieved, Monnet just mentioned that "Realities themselves will enable us to define the political union. The idea is clear: a political Europe will be created by men and women, when the time comes, based on the realities on the ground".[2] We cannot but hope that the crisis we are experiencing is one of these "realities" out of which institutional innovation and political decisions will arise. In any case, there can be only one method to achieve a political union, according to Monnet: it consists of "delegating sovereignty" and "exercising this sovereignty in common".[3] The details of these transfers are of course omitted and in the end the EU remains an unidentified political object. Indeed, most jurists agree today that the EU is a legal construct *sui generis* – which confirms this congenital indetermination and suggests that efforts to define the EU by referring to traditional and proven patterns are probably pointless.

The issue of European constitutionalism paradigmatically illustrates the conceptual, political and legal difficulties we are confronted with when we try to define the EU and to imagine its possible developments and transformations. It emphasizes one of the paradoxes of the European

---

1 "Vers quel aboutissement nous conduit cette nécessité, vers quel type d'Europe, je ne saurais le dire, car il n'est pas possible d'imaginer aujourd'hui les décisions qui pourront être prises dans le contexte de demain. L'essentiel est de s'en tenir aux quelques points fixes sur lesquels nous nous sommes guidés depuis le premier jour: créer progressivement entre les hommes d'Europe le plus vaste intérêt commun géré par des institutions communes démocratiques auxquelles est déléguée la souveraineté nécessaire. Telle est la dynamique qui n'a cessé de fonctionner [...]. Je n'ai jamais douté que ce processus nous mène un jour à des Etats-Unis d'Europe, mais je ne cherche pas à en imaginer aujourd'hui le cadre politique, si imprécis sont les mots à propos desquels on se dispute: confédération ou fédération. Ce que nous préparons, à travers l'action de la Communauté, n'a probablement pas de précédent. Cette communauté est fondée ellemême sur des institutions qu'il faut renforcer, tout en sachant que la véritable autorité politique dont se doteront un jour les démocraties européennes reste à concevoir et à réaliser", Jean Monnet, *Mémoires*, Paris, Fayard, 1976, p. 615-616.

2 "Les réalités elles-mêmes permettront de dégager l'union politique. L'idée est claire: l'Europe politique sera créée par les hommes, le moment venu, à partir des réalités", *ibid.*, p. 505-506.

3 "[...] délégation de souveraineté et exercice en commun de cette souveraineté déléguée", *ibid.*, p. 506.

project: unable to develop without constitutionalizing the European legal framework but unable to find the appropriate manner in which to do so, or the support of the European peoples. These difficulties have historical, conceptual and legal reasons which must be identified and discussed. This was precisely the objective of the seminar on Social Philosophy held at the Inter-University Centre of Dubrovnik in April 2013. The present volume brings together the most significant contributions to this symposium.

The first four contributions address the legal nature and structure of the European Union. *Violeta Beširević* (Union University Law School of Belgrade) shows that EU has an un-codified, evolutive and antirevolutionary constitution, which helps connect the "Politics of Messianism" (J. Weiler) with democracy and positions the EU in a global world. To this end, she outlines the historical context, showing that the words "state" and "constitution" have more or less always been present on the integration agenda. Since a constitution is usually connected with the existence of a state, she then summarizes the different views on legal conceptualization of the EU. Starting from the premise that a constitution can exist without a state, she identifies the core elements of the EU constitution. She then sheds light on some features of internal and external EU constitutionalism which justify her claim that political Messianism in EU integration has been predominantly directed at making democracy the only legitimate form of governance in the EU public order, without a parallel in transnational or international law. *Nenad Dimitrijević* (Central European University of Budapest) focuses on the issue of constitutional identity and asks several related questions: How does constitutional identity relate to pre-political identities? What are the features of constitutional identity? Why does constitutional identity matter, and more particularly how does it relate to democracy and legitimacy? Who is, or who are, the bearers of this identity? N. Dimitrijević emphasizes an important controversial aspect of EU constitutionalism: the identity-specific relationship between historical particularity and constitutional universalism. *Dragica Vujadinović* (Faculty of Law, University of Belgrade) deals with a very similar issue – the concept of European constitutional patriotism – and she underlines the reasons behind its attractiveness. Constitutional patriotism was initially developed in post-war Germany. However, the concept achieved unexpected popularity in the late 1990s when it started being used as a normative model for understanding European identity building – as the civic basis of identification with a supranational political community. The normative and economic attractiveness of the European polity derives from the fact that it is constitutionally capable of enlargement and of "transnational overflowing" towards countries outside of the EU. The attractiveness of the EU comes also from the openness of its constituent power; there is no one unique *demos*, and European *demoi* will have always to negotiate and decide upon what they want and what they do not want to share: the Union does not impose any homogeneity. In his contribution, *Tanasije Marinković* (Faculty of Law, University of Belgrade) addresses the legal nature of European Human Rights Law. While it is undisputed that the formal traits of this law place it within the domain of international law – the High Contracting Parties to the European Convention are states which have accepted the limited jurisdiction of the European Court in their mutual disputes and as concerns individuals' complaints – its essential features, among which the praetorian work of the European Court itself, correspond to the concept of the contemporary judicial review of constitutionality. This paper addresses the complexities of European Human Rights Law due to its dual nature, namely, the international law nature of its basis and the constitutional law nature of its content. Having regard to the level of interplay between these two dimensions, one formal and the other essential, the author concludes that European Human Rights Law is of supranational nature, which is furthermore confirmed by considerations of its normativity.

The following four contributions address the topic of European constitutionalism from a political and philosophical point of view. Dealing with Habermasian political thought, *Gérard Raulet* (Paris-Sorbonne University) argues that Habermas' diagnosis of the withdrawal of the nation state has been widely misunderstood. It must not be forgotten, as Habermas himself reminds us, that the beginning of European public spheres coincided with an affirmation of nationality. Whereas the nation-states of the Old Regime were in fact feudal multinationals, in 1789 and then in 1848 nationalities were associated with the awakening of political public opinion. How does this problem look in a globalized world order in which the role of the sovereign national states is undermined by the structural changes brought about by the reproduction of capital? In his paper, Gérard Raulet examines the different answers given by Habermas in his numerous contributions to the debate about the end-goals of European construction, European identity and European citizenship: "constitutional patriotism"; a "post-state constitutionalism"; but also "solidarity", as the way in which the nation state of the 19th century provided an answer to the need for new identifications; and, not least, the formation of a European people sufficiently homogeneous to form a democratic will. G. Raulet compares these answers to the legal and/or (pseudo) constitutional texts on which a European common will is supposed to be grounded and with the opinions of constitutional lawyers. He concludes that we must deal with two different or even contradictory perspectives: a soft liberal (Anglo-Saxon compatible) and a more radical, more "continental" (French-oriented) conception of democracy and legitimacy. The question is, how does Habermas draw a coherent line between these two distinct approaches, which have influenced his political thinking since its very beginnings in *Strukturwandel der Öffentlichkeit* (1962)? *Alexandre Dupeyrix* (Paris-Sorbonne University) recalls that Kantian cosmopolitanism was for a long time considered the model of supranational citizenship. However historical, social and economic developments that Kant could not foresee oblige us today to rethink his blueprint and to replace it by the concept of "transnational democracy". This contribution sheds light on the conditions required for such a new order and addresses in particular the issues of identity and sovereignty. One of the difficulties the European project seems confronted with is the lack of any European identity. But what kind of identity are we talking about? Cultural or political identity? And how might these two aspects of identity be matched? As for the concept of sovereignty, it seems to be one of the two pillars (with human rights) of a modern democracy: can the EU be a democratic order if sovereignty within the Union is divided, shared or progressively dissolved? *Patrice Canivez* (University of Lille) deals with the type of multiculturalism that is unique to Europe and analyses the relationship between such multiculturalism and the European political integration process. In so doing, he distinguishes between multiculturalism at the level of the European nation-states and multiculturalism at the level of the European Union envisaged as a whole. The analysis considers the diverse aspects of multiculturalism, especially the role of language, religion, history and the different ways in which the process of secularization has developed in the European member states. The chapter notably discusses 1) the distinction made in Canada between multiculturalism and interculturalism and Charles Taylor's suggestion that interculturalism is best suited to European nation-states, 2) the transition, in Habermas' reflections on Europe, from the idea of a post-national European Federation to that of a European transnational democracy. Finally, the chapter relates the question of cultural pluralism in Europe to the much-debated issue of federalism in the European Union. Dealing with the political thought of Jacques Derrida and Jürgen Habermas, *Tonči Valentić* (Zagreb and Ljubljana) claims that Europe is and cannot be anything else but a cosmopolitan project of transnational idea of freedom of citizen and human being in its identity. What is missing today is rather the subject of transnational politics as "metapolitics of advent of freedom of the coming community" (Agamben). Only in this sense can Europe overcome neoliberal technocratic ideology and once again create itself as a project of new power beyond the limitations of nation-states, territorial sovereignty and the limited participation of European citizens in EU politics today.

In the last contribution to this volume, *Maria Găinar* (University of Strasbourg) discusses, in a strictly historical approach, the adoption of the declaration of European identity in December 1973. She argues that this adoption undoubtedly marked the emergence of Europe as a distinctive political entity in the international arena. It is the result of both internal factors (the reflection on European identity initiated in the 1960s) and contextual factors (European reactions to Henry Kissinger's speech on the "Year of Europe", European success with the CSCE process, European concerns vis-à-vis the American-Soviet entente). The declaration entails two dimensions: the affirmation of an independent attitude with regard to different regions in the world and the distinct position of the Nine, with regard to those of the United States and the Soviet Union. Thus, though only momentarily, the Nine make the choice of the "European Europe" and pave the way for progressively "[defining] their identity in relation to other countries or groups of countries".

The editors would like to thank their research group UMR 8138 IRICE and especially its Chair, Eric Bussière, the Excellence Cluster Labex EHNE ("Ecrire une Nouvelle Histoire de l'Europe") and the Doctoral School "Civilisations, Cultures, Littératures et Sociétés" of the University Paris-Sorbonne for their intellectual and financial support.

This volume is dedicated to our colleague and friend Heinz Paetzold, Professor of Philosophy at the University of Kassel and course director of the Dubrovnik seminar, prematurely deceased in 2012.

The Constitution in the European Union

The State of Affairs

Violeta Bešírević

1. Introduction

Today, most Europeans believe that the European Union does not have a constitution and that the idea about having one was buried after the *Constitution for Europe* got double "No" from the French and the Dutch. This view is shared by some academics whose common position is often reduced to a single argument: "no state – no constitution".[1] The German Federal Constitutional Court could not agree more: in its *Maastricht* and *Lisbon* decisions it concluded that the European Union did not have a constitution since it did not have *demos*.[2]

To explain and defend the opposite stance is the main purpose of this article. I intend to show that EU has un-codified, evolutive and antirevolutionary constitution, which helps connecting the Politics of Messianism with democracy and positions EU in the global world.

As to prove this idea, I will not claim that the European constitution mirrors a national constitution in the sense that it is attributable to

---

1 Some German scholars share this view. See e.g. Grimm D., "Does Europe Need a Constitution?" *European Law Journal*, Vol. 1, No. 3, 1995, pp. 282-302. For a discussion on "no state – no constitution" thesis, see e.g. Möllers, C., "Pouvoir Constituant – Constitution – Constitutionalisation", in Bogdandy, A. von and Bast, J. (eds.), *Principles of European Constitutional Law*, Oxford, Oxford University Press, 2011, pp. 169-204; Dominik Hanf, "State and Future of the European Constitution – Improvement or Radical Reform?", in *German Law Journal*, Vol. 2, No. 15, 2001, http://www.germanlawjournal.com/index.php?pageID=11&artID=89.

2 *Manfred Brunner and Others v. The European Union Treaty*, [1994] 1 C.M.L.R. 57, par. 44; the "Lisbon" decision of the German Constitutional Court, BvE 2/08, 2 BvE 5/08, 2 BvR 1010/08, 2 BvR 1022/08, 2 BvR 1259/08 and 2 BvR 182/09, June 30, 2009, par. 277, 279 and 280. For a discussion on *no-demos* thesis see e.g. Weiler J. H. H., 1995, "The State "überalles", Demos, Telos and the German Maastricht Decision", *Jean Monnet Working Papers*, No. 6/95, http://centers.law.nyu.edu/jeanmonnet/archive/papers/95/9506ind.html.

the people, nor that it is a revolutionary product. The reason is simple – European Union is a product of Political Messianism and not of democracy. As Joseph Weiler explains: "in 'political messianism', the justification for action and its mobilizing force, derive not from 'process', as in classical democracy, or from 'result and success', but from the ideal pursued, […]"[3] In the case of Europe, the 'ideal pursued' was that of integration in order to establish long-term peace and reconciliation among former enemies.

Yet, besides pursuing messianic goals, Europe's political elite has for a long time been streaming to root Political Messianism into constitutional democracy, as well. The main vehicle to transform the Community/Union from an international to a constitutional legal order has been constitutionalism.[4] True is, constitutional constraints are by themselves inherently antidemocratic, but constitution is not merely a disabling device but also an enabling one. Constitutions not only limit power and prevent tyranny but also construct power – they establish the rules that help put democracy into effect.[5] In the EU, the efforts to connect Political Messianism and democracy resulted in a rule of law-oriented type of constitution, born in the process of constitutionalization and aimed at submitting public power to law.

The scope of my discussion is limited to identification of the elements of – I am going to call it – EU Constitution, and then to examination to what extent it satisfies the requests of modern constitutionalism. I will start by offering some history to show that a concept of constitution has evolved in response to the constitutional visions of the European integrations. Since a constitution is usually connected with a state, what follows is a brief summary of different views on legal conceptualization of EU. On this point, I will join those who argue that the Union is not a state. However, the next sections will first demonstrate that a constitution can be attributable to the entities different from a state, and second, that democracy is not always the source of the constitutional authority. My next step will be to identify the core elements of the EU constitution. The rest of the discussion will shed light on some features of internal and external EU constitutionalism which justify my claim that Political Messianism in the EU integrations has been predominantly directed at

3 Weiler, J.H.H., "Europe in Crisis – On 'Political Messianism', 'Legitimacy' and the 'Rule of Law'", in *Singapore Journal of Legal Studies*, 2012, pp. 248-268.

4 For more on this process see Craig P., "Constitutions, Constitutionalism and the European Union", in *European Law Journal*, Vol. 7, No. 2, 2001, pp. 125-150.

5 Holmes, S., *Passions and Constraint: On the Theory of Liberal Democracy*, Chicago and London, The University of Chicago Press, 1995, p. 6.

making democracy the only legitimate form of governance in the EU public order, without parallel in transnational or international law.

Now, I turn to history.

2. Some History

There is no doubt that federal Europe has long been a subject of debates about ultimate aims of the European integrations. In 1946, Prime Minister Churchill openly announced: "Our constant aim must be to build and fortify the strength of the United Nations organization. Under and within that world concept we must recreate the European family in a regional structure called – it may be – the United States of Europe and the first practical step will be to form a Council of Europe".[6] Although reference to federation and constitution did not appear in the Schuman Declaration, its architect, Jean Monnet, later explained that establishment of the European federation was a main goal behind the Declaration.[7] At that time, some German politicians and scholars also shared the view. For example, Carlo Schmid, one of the drafters of the German Basic Law, logically argued: "If you want an effective Europe, you have to want a federal state of Europe".[8]

Additionally, the first President of the European Commission, Walter Hallstein, authored the book *The Unfinished Federal State*, in which he advocated federal Europe and clarified that all of the founding fathers of the Community were practically "federalists", who, in 1955, because of a much more ambitious project of a European Defense Community was defeated, turned to the establishment of a surrogate project of European Economic Community, which arguably should have served as the basis for the establishment of the federal community.[9]

In 1966, the dream about federal Europe was interrupted by De Gaulle when he used the "empty chair policy" to protest against the politics of more integration. The result of this conflict is well known: the vision of functional integration, with a primarily economic rationale won, and not the vision of the federal Europe.[10]

6 http://www.coe.int/t/dgal/dit/ilcd/archives/selection/churchill/ZurichSpeech_en.asp.

7 See in Ziller, J., "The Constitutionalization of the European Union: Comparative Perspectives", 55 *Loyola Law Review* 413, 2009, pp. 416-417.

8 Schmid, C., "Deutschland und der Europäische Rat", in *Schriftenreihe des deutschen Rates der europäischen Bewegung*, Vol. 1, cited in Kokott, J., "The Basic Law at 60 – from 1949 to 2009: The Basic Law and Supranational Integration", *German Law Journal*, Vol. 11, p. 104, 2010, fn. 10.

9 Oeter S., "Federalism and Democracy", in Bogdandy, A. von and Bast , J., (eds.), op. cit., p. 57; for more see Hallstein W., *Der unvollendete Bundesstaat. Europäische Erfahrungen und Erkenntnisse*, Düsseldorf, Econ, 1969.

10 Oeter, S., *op.cit.*, pp.57 -58.

During the last decades of the twentieth century, the vision of a federal Europe was set aside. In contrast, an idea of Europe based on common constitution survived in different forms, despite the fact that it was defeated several times. First, in 1984, a draft of the European Constitution made by *Altiero Spinelli* failed, as well as the following effort to make the Maastricht Treaty – a real constitutional instrument.[11] The Amsterdam Treaty was adopted after an attempt to constitutionalize all founding treaties in a common constitution (based on the *Herman Report*) had also failed.[12] The substantial issues which were not resolved in the Amsterdam treaty, like division of competence, democratic legitimacy of the Union, transparency, efficient legislative procedure, including qualified majority voting system, was not resolved either in the Treaty of Nice, adopted in 2001.

At the very beginning of the twenty-first century, German Foreign Minister Joschka Fischer revitalized the debate over the European federation and European Constitution, advocating creation of a loose but sovereign and functional European Federation.[13] Prompted primarily by a then-coming enlargement, in 2001 the European Council adopted Declaration from Laeken, in which it formulated the most important questions of constitutional nature to be resolved at the Convention on the Future of Europe. The decision to rethink the EU legal order in a form of a Constitutional Convention (scheduled for 2002-2003) meant to be a momentous, as was the American Philadelphia Convention of 1787, when the federal American Republic was created.

Yet, although for the first time in history of the European integration the term "constitution" was included in the final document, the European Convention did not produce the same result as the American one. The Treaty Establishing a Constitution for Europe did not envisage federal Europe. Instead, the Constitutional Treaty aimed to legitimize the existed constitutional practices in a non-hierarchical way, meaning that it did not imply strong supremacy of the EU in relation to the member states. Nonetheless, it included the provisions on fundamental rights, chapter on division of powers, as well as the provisions on the EU symbols. Moreover, the fundamental treaties of the EU were named the "Constitution", its regulations – "framework laws" and "laws", the ministers were introduced, and the EU Parliament was designated as an institution of the EU citizens. On one side, the Constitutional Treaty envisaged a number of areas in

---

11 For more see Pernice, I., "The Treaty of Lisbon: Multilevel Constitutionalism in Action", 15 *Columbia Journal of European Law* 349, 2009, pp. 354-356.

12 *Ibid.*, p. 356.

13 His speech is available http://centers.law.nyu.edu/jeanmonnet/search.html?q=Joschka%20Fisher.

which qualified majority was supposed to become a major voting system in the Council. On the other side, it also created a bigger role for the national parliaments in the legislative proceedings of the Union.[14]

In 2004, all EU Member States signed the Constitutional Treaty. The history is yet to determine whether the true reasons for its rejection on referenda in France and the Netherlands were internal economic and political conditions in these countries, a lack of enough information about the constitutional reform, a fear from a super-state or something else. Whichever was the reason, unlike in previous cases, when referendum was reintroduced in some other countries, the force of the double "no" was so convincing, that organizing a new referendum in France and the Netherlands was out of consideration.[15]

Instead, the European political elite focused on drafting a new Reform Treaty (later known as the Lisbon Treaty), and openly promised that "the constitutional concept" is abandoned, and that the parts of the future Treaty – "the *TEU* and the *Treaty on Functioning of the Union* will not have a constitutional character."[16] However, behind the scene, they had something different in mind: the Lisbon Treaty should have preserved constitutional practices as defined in the abandoned Constitutional Treaty in a way which would allow referendum in the Member States to be avoided. German Chancellor, Angela Merkel, has openly admitted this fact: "My friend Sarkozy and I have suggested to call it not a Constitution but a Reform Treaty because only then another French referendum could be avoided".[17]

The result of the political manoeuver is the following: The Lisbon Treaty comprises of two treaties amending the previously existing EU fundamental treaties. Constitutional terminology as "constitution", "law", "framework law", "the Minister of Foreign affairs", were removed from the text, as well as the Union symbols. The provision regarding the supremacy of the EU law was moved from the main text into the declaration included in the Final Act.[18] The EU Charter of Fundamental Rights was also removed from the main text. However, Article 6 of the present EU

---

14 For a discussion see Pernice, I., *op. cit.*, pp. 370-371.

15 For more see Búrca G. de, "If at First You Don't Succeed: Vote, Vote Again: Analyzing the Second Referendum Phenomenon in EU Treaty Change", 33 *Fordham International Law Journal* 1472, 2010, pp. 1472-1489.

16 See Council of the European Union, *IGC 2007 Mandate*, 11218/07, Brussels, 26 June 2007 http://register.consilium.europa.eu/pdf/en/07/st11/st11218.en07.pdf.

17 See in Brunkhorst, H., "The Future of the European Constitution", in Closa, C. (ed.), *The Lisbon Treaty and National Constitutions. Europeanization and Democratic Implications*, ARENA Report No. 3/09, RECON Report No. 9, Oslo, 2009, p. 168.

18 See 17. Declaration concerning primacy, annexed to the Final Act (2007/C 306/02).

Treaty referrers to the Charter and declares that it has the same binding force as the treaties composing the Lisbon Treaty.[19]

This short journey through the history of EU integrations cannot be ended without referring to the Court of Justice of the EU, and its major court – the Court of Justice, initially known as the European Court of Justice (ECJ). Among the members of EU academia, there is a common narrative that the ECJ began to build, through its case law, a constitutionalized, pro-federal-legal order back in 1960s, in order to save the integration process, jammed due to De Gaulle's politics of empty chair.[20] As I will show later, the ECJ is a principal actor in introducing and supporting the migration of constitutional ideas into the EU.

In sum, from the very beginning, aspirations and conversations among different actors involved in the European integrations, resulted in constitutional rather than international law practices. This begs the question of the EU conceptualization.

3. State or Non-State Polity?

The conceptualization of the Union has been for quite some time a highly topical subject of academic debates. Generally, a different characterization of the legal nature of the EU can be broken under three main categories.

First, some authors claim that the EU is a treaty based intergovernmental organization, whose member states are still primarily interested and obliged to achieve national interests. Andrew Moravcsik, the well-known follower of this approach, argues that the best confirmation of this theory is a failure of the Constitutional Treaty, which supposed to launch a European super-state.[21]

Second, many argue that the EU is a state-like entity. There is a long-time tendency to discuss relations among the Community/Union, national governments and EU citizens in terms of federation, despite the fact that the European polity possesses more confederative than federative characteristics. Among those who support state-like approach, some claim that the EU has already acquired characteristics of a federal state.[22] Such

---

[19] For more on the Lisbon Treaty see e.g. Craig, P., *The Lisbon Treaty: Law, Politics, and Treaty Reform*, Oxford, Oxford University Press, 2010.

[20] For a discussion, see Laurence, H. and Karen, A., "Legitimacy and Lawmaking: A Tale of Three International Courts", 14 Theoretical Inquiries in Law 479, 2013, pp. 487-493.

[21] Moravcsik, A., "What Can We Learn from the Collapse of the European Constitutional Project?" *Politische Vierteljahresschrift*, 2006, Vol. 47, No. 2, pp. 219-241.

[22] See e.g. Denis J., "Fearing Federalism's Failure: Subsidiarity in the European Union", 44 *American Journal of Comparative Law* 537, 1996.

arguments first appeared in the aftermath the Maastricht Treaty, and were drawn from institutional designs of a common foreign and security policy, protection of human rights, common currency, the EU citizenship, the EU Parliament, the EU Central Bank, as well as from the ECJ influential jurisprudence.[23] Similar arguments were offered after the Lisbon Treaty was adopted. European federalists assert that the European integrations will end up in the creation of the Union of the European States when Member States accept completely to delegate its sovereign jurisdiction in the area of foreign and security affairs to the Union and when the Council gives up the central role it now plays in the EU.[24]

Third, many authors support "something else" approach and commonly refer to the Union's *sui generis* nature. For example, starting from the EU common legal order, territory and citizenship, Armin von Bogdandy claimed that the Maastricht Treaty created a new form of political governance, whose legal nature was best described as "supranational federation", distinguishable from a classic federation, but which existed parallel to it.[25] Weiler understands the present Union in terms of polity based on "constitutional tolerance".[26] Ignolf Pernice explains that the Lisbon Treaty has consolidated multilevel constitutional structure of a new kind, based upon functioning democratic Member States, complementary to them, and binding them together in a supranational unit without itself being a state or aiming at statehood.[27]

Finally, some authors claim that the EU is the best understood in a way distinct from both national and supranational versions of single *demos*. Kalypso Nikolaidis speaks about *demoicracy* and defines the European Union as "a Union of peoples, understood both as states and as citizens, who govern together but not as one".[28] The EU *demoicracy* is not a state nor supranational entity. It is legitimized by pluralism of *demoi*.

---

23 *Ibid.*, p. 539.

24 Mancini, G.F., "Europe: The Case for Statehood", *European Law Journal*, Vol. 4, No. 1, 1998, pp. 29-42.

25 Bogdandy, A. von, "The European Union as a Supranational Federation: A Conceptual Attempt in the Light of the Amsterdam Treaty", 6 *Columbia Journal of European Law* 27, 2000, pp. 27-54.

26 Weiler, J.H.H., "Federalism Without Constitutionalism: Europe's Sonderweg", in Nicolaïdis, K. and Howse, R. (eds.), *The Federal Vision: Legitimacy and Levels of Governance in the United States and the European Union*, Oxford, Oxford University Press, 2001, pp. 54-70.

27 Pernice, I., *op. cit.*, pp. 350-351, 406-407.

28 Nicolaïdis, K., "The Idea of European Demoicracy", in Dickson, J., and Eleftheriadis, P. (eds.), *Philosophical Foundations of European Union Law*, Oxford, Oxford University Press, 2012, pp. 247-274.

Now, suppose that Union is not a state. Does this mean that it does not have a constitution? I turn now to this issue.

4. A Short Reminder on Different Constitutional Traditions

Usually, existence of the constitution is linked to the existence of the state. However, this is not a rule. Some international organizations, including the ILO, UNESCO and the UN FAO, have constitutions although they are not the states. Be that as it may, this argument bears no importance in this discussion, because the international organizations are not empowered to exercise legislative and executive powers, producing direct consequences for the individuals, which is exactly what Union does. Today, EU performs important political, economic and social functions, among which those in the field of freedom, security and justice deserve to be particularly emphasized.[29] Accordingly, what has to be limited at the Union level is not a state but public power.[30]

The issue whether the Union has a constitution became the subject of the academic interest after the German Constitutional Court in its *Maastricht* decision concluded that Union did not have *demos* and therefore it lacked a constitutional document (*no-demos* thesis).[31] According to the Court, the EU fundamental treaties composing the Maastricht Treaty were not constitutional instruments but international treaties, whose masters were the Member States.[32] In the discussion that followed, some have defended the Court's arguments,[33] while others endorsed the post-state and post-national perspective, emphasizing that constitutions could exist on transnational level, including the Union itself.[34]

Those who claim that a constitution can only be attached to the existence of democratic, homogeneous *pouvoir constituant* pursue an argument that there is no constitution without a state. Their claim is based on the so-called power-limiting or order-founding constitutional tradition, characterized by the existence of revolutionary constitution, aimed at founding an entirely new order and limiting government for the purpose

---

29 Craig, P., and Búrca G. de, *EU Law: Text, Cases, and Materials*, Oxford, Oxford University Press, 2011, p. 155.

30 Grimm, D., "Types of Constitutions", in Rosenfeld, M., and Sajó, A. (eds.), *The Oxford Handbook of Comparative Constitutional Law*, Oxford, Oxford University Press, 2012, p. 130.

31 *Manfred Brunner and Others v. The European Union Treaty*, par. 44.

32 *Ibid.*, par. 55, 77.

33 See e.g. Grimm, D., "Does Europe Need a Constitution?", *op. cit.*

34 Habermas, J., "Remarks on Dieter Grimm's 'Does Europe Need a Constitution?'", *European Law Journal*, Vol. 1, No. 3, 1995, pp. 303-307.

of preserving individual freedom. The American and the French constitutional traditions are cases at point.[35]

Remarkably, this approach overlooks the existence of, what Möllers calls, "power-shaping" constitutional tradition, which is not aimed at creating a new political order, but at legalization or juridification of already existing one.[36] In this tradition, a constitution does not constitute a new polity but rather aims at limiting a pre-democratic or already existing sovereign power through legal rules. Although they differ in details, the power-shaping constitutional tradition is typically connected with England and Germany.[37]

Now, the EU constitutional tradition shares with German and Britain constitutional tradition a lack of revolutionary moment and an idea of evolutional constitutionalism. Although even today it is without a written constitutional instrument, Great Britain does not lack a constitution – its Constitution has been constantly developed and apprehended as an evolutionary process of political practices. The German example also testifies that democracy has not always been a starting point in building a new polity. Constitutional norms have its historical source in constitutional treaties of the ninetieth century that served as constitutions of the first German nation-state.[38] They were concluded by sovereign states and did not create a new order, but rather, the sovereign states transferred a part of their sovereign powers to the common institutions.[39] Historically, the Union emerged in a similar manner.

There is further wrinkle here. A nation-state oriented constitutionalism is usually associated with France, but the truth is, as Hannah Arendt convincingly argued, that a notion of democratic homogeneity was not a part of the French Revolution.[40] As mentioned earlier, neither the German constitutional history is familiar with *le pouvoir constituant*, nor is the British constitutional tradition familiar with a strong concept of the state.[41] Moreover, accepting the argument of the German Constitutional Court, advanced in its *Lisbon* decision, that existence of homogenous *demos*, who forms *le pouvoir constituant* and who exercise its power on free and democratic elections based on equal rights for all voters, provide

35 Möllers, C., *op. cit.*, pp. 171-173, 179.
36 *Ibid.*, p. 172.
37 *Ibid.*, pp. 172-176.
38 *Ibid.*, p. 176.
39 *Ibid.*
40 Arendt H., *On Revolution*, London, Penguin Books, 1990.
41 Möllers C., *op. cit.*, p. 179.

necessary legitimization for a state,[42] means denying constitutional character of many states, including, for example, the Second German Empire.[43] Not to mention that even today's Germany, as a federal state, does not function on the principle of equal rights for all voters. All in all, the idea of ultimate connection between constitution and a nation-state can hardly be found in the history of the European states.

In short, the fact that the current funding document of the EU is termed the Lisbon Treaty, as well as the fact that it lacks democratic legitimization, does not necessarily imply a conclusion that the EU does not have constitution. Democracy is not a necessary precondition for a constitution to emerge: constitutional norms can be shaped in the context of the "rule of law constitutionalism" (Brunkhorst), in which constitutional standards steam from the process of juridification of the public power.

This brings me to the final and the most basic problem: namely, what remains to be proven is that the exercise of public power at the Union level has been organized and limited in a way usually crafted by a constitution.

5. The Sources of EU Constitutional Authority

A test to explore whether the EU has a constitution is the French revolutionary Declaration, which declared civil rights and in Article 16 proclaimed "a society in which the observance of the law is not assured, nor the separation of powers defined, has no constitution at all." Under this test, the existence of the EU un-codified constitution receives its confirmation. A short explanation is the following.

It is worth repeating that the Lisbon Treaty and its relevant protocols guarantee the rule of law and organize exercise of the public power by providing institutional balance among Union institutions, division of powers between the Union and the Member States, as well as hierarchy of legal norms. Second, the EU Charter on Fundamental Rights, attached to the Lisbon Treaty, has become legally binding for all Member States and does not represent any more only a set of empty rights. The Lisbon Treaty also recognizes the Union as an autonomous legal personality. Based on these facts, I will join Habermas who argues that the treaties forming the Lisbon Treaty have become a foundation of a political community with a constitution of its own.[44]

---

42 The *Lisbon* decision, par. 277, 279 and 280.

43 Brunkhorst H., "Demokratija shvaćena ozbiljno: Evropa posle propasti ustava", *Anali Pravnog fakulteta u Beogradu*, No. 2, 2005, pp. 5-19.

44 Habermas, J., "The Crisis of the European Union in the Light of a Constitutionalization of International Law", *European Journal of International Law*, Vol. 23, No. 2, 2013, p. 342. Even before the adoption of the Lisbon Treaty, some claimed that the EU

Yet, there is more to add. The EU constitutional standards steam also from the jurisprudence of the ECJ. As Habermas notes, its principal role to interpret the founding treaties in absence of the published preparatory documents, made the ECJ deal constantly with the question which Madison faced in 1787, during foundation of the US: "can a federation of member states with democratic constitutions satisfy the conditions of democratic legitimation, without the national level being clearly subordinated to the federal level, as it is in the federal state?"[45] In the foundational Van *Gend en Loos* case, decided over forty years ago, the ECJ declared the autonomy of the Community legal order, underlining its *sui generis* character.[46] In the subsequent cases, it ruled that the Community treaties constituted the constitutional charter of the Community, based on the rule of law.[47] In the presence of a legislative gap, the ECJ has also secured direct effect and supremacy of EU law in the Member States.[48] This Court was also very influential in developing human rights standards within the EU legal order, although they were completely omitted in the foundational Communities treaties concluded in 1950s. Lastly, but not less importantly, the ECJ has asserted its sweeping power of judicial review several times, last time in the first *Kadi* judgment, delivered in 2008, when it asserted that: "Community is based on the rule of law, inasmuch as neither its Member States non its institutions can avoid review of the conformity of their acts with the basic constitutional charter, the Community Treaty [...]."[49]

Finally, EU constitutional standards also originate from the Member States' constitutional orders. The Community/Union's human rights policy has derived from this source. Despite their divergence, von Bogdandy claims that dependence of the Union's constitution on the Member States' constitutions is greater in law and in fact than that of a federal state on its constituent states.[50]

already had a *de facto* constitution (Treaty of Rome), which had served it well. See Moravcsik, A., *op. cit.*, p. 220.

45 Habermas, J., "The Crisis of the European Union in the Light of a Constitutionalization of International Law", *op. cit.*, p. 342.

46 ECJ: European Court of Justice, case – EUECJ R-26/62, *NV Algemene Transport- en Expeditie Onderneming Van Gend en Loos v. Nederlandse Administratie der Belastingen*, CMLR 105, [1963] ECR 1.

47 ECJ: European Court of Justice, case – 294/83 *Partiécologiste "Les Verts" v. European Parliament*, [1986] ECR 1339.

48 *Van Gend en Loos*, *op. cit.*; ECJ: European Court of Justice, case-6/64, *Costa v. ENEL*, [1964] ECR 585.

49 ECJ: European Court of Justice, Joined Cases C-402/05 P and C-415/05 P, *Yassin Abdullah Kadi and Al Barakaat International Foundation v. Council of the European Union and Commission of the European Communities*, [2008] ECR I-6351. Further in the text: *Kadi I.*

50 Bogdandy, A. von, "Founding Principles", in Bogdandy, A. von and Bast, J. (eds.), *op. cit.*, p. 39.

He also warns that Member States' constitutions can hardly be adequately grasped without resource to the Union's constitution any more, since they no longer constitutionalize all public power in their scope of application.[51]

The foundations of this EU un-codified, complicated and pretty non-transparent constitutional structure have been explained by several constitutional theories, including theories on constitutional pluralism, constitutional synthesis, multilevel-constitutionalism and constitutional tolerance.[52]

The quality of EU constitutionalism has been target of a broad criticism. In the rest of my discussion, I will revisit some aspects of EU constitutionalism that help sustain the EU constitutional authority.

6. Internal Aspects of EU Constitutionalism: Moving Beyond Generalization

In principle, modern constitutionalism requires imposing limits on the powers of the government, loyalty to the rule of law and protection of fundamental rights.[53] In pursuing these ideas, the actors participating in constitutionalization of the Community/Union have not succeeded in generating coherent constitutional standards that would well fit in a contemporary understanding of constitutional democracy. Put simply, while the Community/Union was mostly responsive to the ideas of promoting the rule of law and securing the recognition of fundamental rights, it did not manage to consolidate its authority through the lens of democratic-decision making. Before tackling the key problem of the democratic deficit, I will briefly mention the Union's most important achievements in the human rights field.

The EU may not originate as a human rights organization, yet it nonetheless has managed to achieve an impressive record in developing human rights protection – from silence in the treaties establishing the Communities in 1950s, to the legally binding EU Charter of Fundamental Rights, attached to the 2009 Lisbon Treaty. Beside the Charter, the general principles of EU law, drawing from national constitutional traditions, and international treaties signed by the Member States, the most important being the European Convention for the Protection of Human Rights

51 *Ibid.*

52 For a discussion see e.g. Fossum, J. E. and Menéndez, J. A., "The Theory of Constitutional Synthesis: A Constitutional Theory for a Democratic European Union", *RECON On Line Working Paper*, 2010/25, http://www.reconproject.eu/main.php/RECON_wp_1025.pdf?fileitem=3653824.

53 For more see e.g. Rosenfeld, M., "The Rule of Law and the Legitimacy of Constitutional Democracy", 74 *Southern California Law Review* 1307, 2001.

and Fundamental Freedoms (ECHR), are also sources of the rights protection in the Union. Moreover, the EU is soon to access to the ECHR itself.[54] Finally, to this list of achievements, a clear inclination of the ECJ to engage substantially in human rights adjudication, particularly in the area of discrimination, data protection, privacy and "war against terrorism", should be added. However, one should not forget that despite settled case law, for a long time some were sceptical towards the quality of the rights protection within the EU legal order, asserting that the ECJ did not distinguish human rights from fundamental market freedoms.[55] Nevertheless, the ECJ has managed to mitigate this scepticism when, in a series of its antiterrorism decisions delivered in the post 9/11 period, it struck down a number of EU measures for violating a variety of fundamental rights, including due process rights and the right to property.[56]

Although it is reasonable to wonder whether EU commitments to human rights amounts to something more than self-legitimizing politics, which is also, undeniably, still subject of many flows, EU institutional and policy developments in the field of human rights are less contested than constitutional practices aimed at limiting the powers of its institutions. Therefore, I turn now to this issue.

A major argument in favour of EU reduced constitutionalism steams from a lack of democratic legitimacy. However, the history of the European integrations indicates that many efforts have been undertaken to mitigate this state of affairs. The latest, included in the Lisbon Treaty, are aimed at improving quality of representative and participatory democracy in the Union, as well as at increasing the role of the national parliaments in the Union's decision-making proceedings. Consider the following.

The Lisbon Treaty is drafted to follow the usual qualities of representative democracy. Article 10 of the TEU determines that at the Union level citizens are directly represented in the European Parliament, and indirectly represented in the European Council and in the Council through their Member States representatives (who are democratically accountable either to their national Parliaments or to their citizens).

Measured by usual democratic standards, representative democracy in the Union reflects the following tendencies. On one hand, the European

---

54 The final version of the draft agreement on Accession of the EU to ECHR was adopted on April 5, 2013.

55 Kühling J., "Fundamental Rights", in Bogdandy A. von and Bast J. (eds.), *op. cit.*, pp. 479-514; Kingreen, T., "Fundamental Freedoms", in Bogdandy A. von and Bast J. (eds.), *op. cit.*, pp. 515-549; Möllers, C., *op. cit.*, p. 182.

56 For a discussion see Tridimas, T., "Terrorism and ECJ: Empowerment and Democracy in the EC Legal Order", *European Law Review*, Vol. 34, No. 1, 2009, pp. 103-126.

Parliament is not a sovereign legislator whose word is final; it is not a parliament that supports governing majority nor does it have majority coalition. Other political institutions are still not fully responsible to it for all acts they adopt, nor the adaption of all important decisions requests the European Parliament's approval. On the other hand, its legislative, supervisory and budgetary powers have increased over time, as has its power over the appointment of the Commission.[57]

To remind, before the adoption of the European Single Act in 1986, the Parliament was given a few powers, including consultative and supervisory, but not legislative power and therefore was labelled as "multilingual talking shop". Under the Maastricht Treaty, it got the equal role in the legislative making as the Council. The Lisbon Treaty secures its participation as an equal partner in the ordinary legislative proceedings (subject to the Commission's initiations), which covers approximately 44 areas, including agriculture, services, immigration, structural funds, etc.[58] Moreover, the European Parliament has a status of veto player over delegated acts adopted by the Commission with an aim to implement EU regulations in more details.[59] Apart from a major role in the legislative process, the budgetary function that it shares with the Council, the Parliament uses very tactically to influence a change in the institutional balance and emphasize its representative role.

At this point, it is necessary to underline that democratic legitimacy of the Union legislative acts, although of a limited nature, springs from the described institutional balance, which in the Union serves as an autonomous version of separation of powers principle.[60] The readiness of the Members States to increase legislative powers of the European Parliament, although deeply controversial, has produced two important consequences. First, the increased capacity of the European Parliament to influence EU policy-making has weakened the democratic deficit argument. Second, the Parliament now functions as mechanism to compensate for domestic de-parlamentarisation, since transfer of sectorial policy decisions to the EU level has undermined the power of domestic parliaments to control and influence their governments in EU policy-making.[61]

---

57 For similar view see Corbett, R., Jacobs, F. and Shackleton, M., *The European Parliament*, (7th ed.), London, John Harper Publishing, 2007, p. 245.

58 For a detail overview see Craig, P. and Búrca, G. de, *op. cit.*, pp. 51-58.

59 *Ibid.*, p. 54.

60 ECJ: European Court of Justice, case – 138/79, *Roquette Frères v. Council of the European Communities*, [1980] ECR 3333.

61 Auel K. and Rittberger B., "Fluctuant necmerguntur. The European Parliament, National Parliaments, and European Integration", in Richardson J. (ed.), *European Union: Power and Policy-Making*, 3rd ed., London, Routledge, 2006, pp. 136-137.

Besides representative democracy, the Lisbon Treaty speaks also about participatory democracy. Even before it became law, some elements of the participatory democracy were to be found in EU law.[62] The novelty brought by the Lisbon Treaty is the citizens' initiative of inviting the European Commission to submit a legislative proposal for adoption. Yet, its effects remain to be seen.

Finally, the Lisbon Treaty has improved EU democratic credentials by reserving more space for the national parliaments in the EU decision-making process. This argument calls for further explanation.

An optimal version of incorporating the national parliaments within the EU institutional system through a new parliamentary Chamber or European Senate, although frequently discussed, has never come to fruition.[63] Nonetheless, under the Lisbon Treaty, the national parliaments have acquired an opportunity to exercise a more efficient control over the adoption of some European acts, by supervising the implementation of the subsidiarity principle.[64] This, so-called "early warning mechanism", requests that the Commission sends all legislative proposals to the national parliaments at the same time as to the Union institutions, and informs them about any views and positions taken by the Union with regard to such proposals.[65] The national parliaments may within 8 weeks send to the Union institutions a reasoned opinion as to why they consider that the proposal does not comply with subsidiarity.[66] Although, in principle, it will be difficult to ensure the required number of national parliaments to present reasoned opinion in relation to the same EU measure, so as to compel the Commission to review or even to withdraw the proposal, the Commission is likely to take seriously any such opinion, particularly if it originates from a larger Member State.[67] One should not forget that,

62 See e.g. ECJ: European Court of Justice, case C-49/88, *Al-Jubail Fertilizer Company (Samad) and Saudi Arabian Fertilizer Company (Safco) v. Council of the European Communities*, [1991] ECR I-03187; case – T-410/06, *Foshan City Nanhai Golden Step Industrial Co., Ltd v. Council of the European Union*, [2010] ECR II-00879; see also Article 42 of the EU Charter on Fundamental Rights.

63 Witte, B. de, "The Lisbon Treaty and the National Constitutions. More or Less Europeanization?", in Closa, C. (ed.), 2009, *op. cit.*, p. 38.

64 The issue is regulated by the Protocol on the Application of the Principles of Subsidiarity and Proportionality (Protocol on Subsidiarity) and the Protocol on the Role of National Parliaments in the EU (Protocol on National Parliaments). Both protocols are annexed to the Lisbon Treaty.

65 See Article 4 of the Protocol on Subsidiarity and Article 2 of the Protocol on National Parliaments.

66 See Article 6 of the Protocol on Subsidiarity and Article 4 of the Protocol on National Parliaments.

67 Craig, P. and Búrca, G. de, *op. cit.*, p. 97.

according to the same system and with the extended period for consideration (not 8 weeks but 6 months), national parliaments are directly involved in the procedures regarding the accession of new member states and amending the founding treaties.[68]

The "early warning mechanism" is one of the clearest examples by which the Union deviates from the classical model of international organization. It sheds additional lights on EU multilevel constitutional structure, for the mechanism requires cooperation not only between Union and national parliaments, but also between national parliaments themselves.[69] First, although, as a rule, a national parliament does not have an obligation to take the position with regard to particular legislative proposal, the non-participation of one or more parliaments would weaken the role of others, because the national parliaments' veto power depends on the number of parliaments expressing the negative opinion.[70] Accordingly, as Bruno de Witte, rightly notes, we are dealing here with the obligation of the national parliaments rather than with the model of information.[71] Second, the obligation triggers the work of many national institutions, including governments, domestic parliamentary committees, and national parliaments themselves. Third, the application of the early warning mechanism has provoked in the Member States either constitutional changes (in France) or legislative changes concerning functioning of the national parliaments.[72]

To conclude. The Lisbon Treaty represents an attempt to legitimize European Union in a way that brings Union closer to democracy. Yet, despite some improvement in democratic practices, it cannot be repeated often enough that Union still suffers from democratic deficit. The voters still cannot change the executives, nor can determine, by their vote, composition of the EU institutions – among three institutions performing legislative function – the only one directly elected is the European Parliament. Starting from the premise that the idea of democracy makes sense only to the extent to which political parties are allowed to fight over power,[73] the absence of genuine European parties makes already fragile democratic credentials more obvious. Finally, the lack of or weakness of

---

68 Articles 48 and 49 of the TEU.

69 Pernice, I., *op. cit.*, p. 26.

70 Witte, B. de, *op. cit.*, p. 39.

71 *Ibid.*

72 *Ibid.*, pp. 39-40.

73 Pildes, R., "Political Parties and Constitutionalism", in Ginsburg T. and Dixon R. (eds.), Comparative Constitutional Law, Edward Edgar Publishing, Cheltenham, 2011, p. 254.

a European *demos*, understood as a "political community of common attachment and engagement",[74] also explains why the Union is commonly seen as a democratic deficit setting.

However, pitting the EU democratic credentials against the democratic credentials of today's constitutional democracies may soften this conclusion. Constitutionalism and democracy are not about to triumph across the globe. Executives tend to dominate most modern domestic politics. Moreover, even in the old democracies, the classical tenets of constitutionalism – the rule of law, separation of powers and human rights protection – have been severely challenged by the "war on terrorism", the fight against illegal migrants and the financial meltdown. Examined through these lenses, usual generalization of EU constitutionalism and democracy appear less compelling. A discussion on EU judicial politics in human rights protection, further underlines this point.

7. External Aspect of EU Constitutionalism: Some Reflections on the *Kadi I* Judgment

While the discussion about internal aspects of EU constitutionalism has shown that the Union's major problem is a lack of consolidated democratic procedures, the discussion that follows will reveal that its external aspects, founded on the rule of law and human rights politics, appear to be constructed on a much more consolidated basis. A credit for that goes almost exclusively to the ECJ.

For the purpose of this discussion, the ECJ's antiterrorism jurisprudence, in particular, the decision in *Kadi I* case, delivered in 2008, bears particular importance, because it improves the quality of EU human rights protection and underlines external dimensions of the European constitutionalism.

Facts first. In the case of *Kadi I*, a Saudi Arabian national, Yassin A. Kadi, and the Al Barakaat International Foundation, both with substantial assets in the EU, brought in front of the ECJ an action for the annulment of several EU regulations, adopted to implement a series of UN Security Council resolutions concerning the fight against international terrorism.[75] Enacted under the Chapter VII of the UN Charter, the Security Council resolutions required for all states to take measures to freeze the funds and other financial assets of individuals and entities associated with Osama

74 Walker, N., "The Migration of Constitutional Ideas and the Migration of the Constitutional Idea: the Case of the EU", in *The Migration of Constitutional Ideas*, Choudhry, S. (ed.), Cambridge, Cambridge University Press, 2006, p. 322.

75 *Kadi I*, par. 16-45.

bin Laden, Al-Qaeda network and the Taliban.[76] The Sanction Committee of the Security Council adopted and amended many times the list containing the names of the persons and entities whose funds were to be frozen. To this aim, and in accordance with the Security Council resolutions, several EU regulations were adopted, with direct legal effect in the national legal systems of all EU Members States. Subsequently, both Kadi and the Al Barakaat were listed in the annex to the regulations as suspected of ties with terrorism. Therefore, their funds and financial assets in EU were frozen.[77]

Before the Court of First Instance (now the General Court), they claimed the contested EU regulations violated their fundamental rights, in particular, the right to property, the right to a fair hearing and the right to judicial remedy, all well-established in the ECJ's jurisprudence to the effect that fundamental rights recognized and guaranteed by the constitutions of the Member States, and especially those provided in the ECHR, formed an integral part of the Union legal order.[78]

The first instance judgments, delivered by the General Court, rejected all Kadi's and the Al Barakaat's claims.[79] However, in reversing, the Grand Chamber in the second instance judgment accentuated autonomy, authority and separateness of the EU from the international legal order, making thereby an earthquake in international law.

Thus, the ECJ annulled the EU regulations in so far as they imposed sanctions on the claimants, finding that the regulations constituted unjustified restriction of their right to be heard, the right to an effective legal remedy and the right to property.[80] However, the Court did not stop here. It ruled that the obligations imposed by international treaty could not have the effect of prejudicing the constitutional principles of the European

---

[76] See the UN Security Council resolutions No. 1267 (1999), 1333 (2000), 1390 (2002), 1452 (2002), and 1455 (2003).

[77] *Kadi I*, par. 39-40.

[78] At that time, the Lisbon Treaty, referring to legally binding EU Charter on Fundamental Rights, was not yet into force.

[79] ECJ: European Court of Justice, case T-315/0, *Yassin Abdullah Kadi v. Council of the European Union and Commission of the European Communities*, [2005] ECR II-03649; case T-306/01, *Ahmed Ali Yusuf and Al Barakaat International Foundation v. Council of the European Union and Commission of the European Communities*, [2005] ECR II-3533.

[80] *Kadi I*, par. 333-353, 357-372. In the following cases, the ECJ continued to rule in favor of *Yassin Abdullah Kadi*. See the Judgment of the General Court, case – T-85/09, *Yassin Abdullah Kadi v. European Commission*, [2010] ECR II-05177 (*Kadi II*); ECJ: European Court of Justice, Joined Cases C-584/10 P, C-593/10 P and C-595/10 P, *Commission, Council, United Kingdom v Yassin Abdullah Kadi*, [2013] not yet reported.

Community Treaty (specifically – allocation of powers and human rights standards), and reaffirmed its earlier finding that the EU autonomous legal system is based on the rule of law.[81] The most striking part of the judgment deals with the status of the UN Charter within the EU legal order in which the Court treated "all EU recognized 'fundamental rights' as belonging to normatively superior category". By doing so, the ECJ in *Kadi I* significantly challenged the arguments about reduced constitutionalism at the Community/Union level.[82]

Now, the issue is why the ECJ has decided in *Kadi I* not only to consolidate EU constitutional order, but also to present the vision of its superiority, to which international law – is external and subordinate? A less ambitious court would have chosen to act more flexible. For example, it would have borrowed the *Solange* doctrine from the German Constitutional Court, established in the conflict over human rights protection between that Court and the ECJ itself, at the time when the Community suffered from deficiency in human rights protection.[83] The German Constitutional Court ruled in a compromising manner, determining that the Community legal order and the German legal order stood in "mutually disciplining relation" (Weiler), meaning that the Court would examine the compatibility of EU legislation with fundamental rights standards guaranteed in Germany as long as effective protection was missing at the Community level.[84] In contrast, the ECJ in *Kadi I* has failed to use the situation of a clear inconformity of the UN Security Council antiterrorist resolutions with universally recognized human rights standards, as an opportunity to influence consolidation of universal mechanisms for the human rights protection. Instead, it decided to distance the EU from the international politics tolerant to human rights abuses.

De Búrca explains that the Court's approached in the *Kadi I* judgment has more in common with the U.S. long-standing general distrust towards international law, than with a general attitude of EU, which has been for a long time associated with respect and fidelity to international

81 *Ibid.*, par. 281, 282, 285.

82 Búrca, G. de, "The ECJ and the International Legal Order: a Re-Evaluation", in Búrca, G. de and Weiler, J.H.H. (eds.), *The Worlds of European Constitutionalism*, Cambridge, Cambridge University Press, 2012, p. 121.

83 Several authors refer to this possibility including Gráinne De Búrca. *Ibid.*, pp. 141-143.

84 *Internationale Handelsgesellschaft von Einfuhr- und Vorratsstelle für Getreide und Futtermittel*, (*Solange I*), BVerfGE 37, 271 [1974] CMLR 540. In the mid 1980s, the German Constitutional Court ruled that the need for such control no longer existed for human rights protection acquired meaningful status at the Community level. *Solange II*, BVerfGE 73, 339, [1987] 3 CMLR 225.

law and its institutions.[85] The real issue, therefore, is – why did in *Kadi I* the Court choose to deviate from the Union's general respect for international law? Among many speculations, one deserves particular attention: a strict primacy and sovereignty language in *Kadi I* coincides with the EU efforts to promote itself as an international actor at the global stage of international relations, not less significant than the US, Russia and China.[86] Furthermore, Weiler convincingly argues that *Kadi I* also reflects a need of Europe to distance itself from Asia/Muslim bloc in the world of global politics.[87]

It is for all these reasons reasonable to claim that the EU constitutional authority also serves to position EU in the world of global governance.

8. Conclusions

My first aim in this discussion was to show that EU lives under the constitution. To insist on its blueprint, I have followed eye-catching metaphor: "if it looks, walks, and quacks like a duck, then it is probably a duck." In other words, when placed against the background of Article 16 of the French revolutionary Declaration, the EU legal order manifests the features of a constitution, progressively developed to root Political Messianism into democracy and position EU in the global order. The EU constitution denies the premise that a constitution is always philosophical construct, and fits well into argumentation that, in modern times, constitutional framework emanates from political decision-making, and not from pre-established truth.[88]

My second aim was to assess to what extent EU constitutional standards satisfied the requests of modern constitutionalism, generally understood as a set of limits on the powers of the government and adherence to the rule of law and the protection of human rights. The discussion has revealed that EU's present constitutional achievements can be identified with the rule of law environment and human rights recognition, while a lack of connection between political power and electoral accountability is still missing constitutional feature. The fact that EU democratic defects appear less visible when pitted against the defects of national constitutional systems can only partially alleviate weaknesses of EU democratic credentials.

85 Búrca, G. de, "The ECJ and the International Legal Order: a Re-Evaluation", pp. 142-145.

86 Búrca, G. de and Weiler, J.H.H., *op. cit.*, p. 280.

87 *Ibid.*

88 Grimm, D., "Types of Constitutions", *op. cit.*, p. 104.

The existence of the EU constitution and trust in the responsiveness of the EU constitutional order are two different issues. "Democratic constitutionalism" underlines that constitutional authority is based on both its democratic responsiveness and its legitimacy as a law.[89] For the time being, European citizens do not perceive the existing un-codified EU Constitution as law nor its standards as distinct from everyday politics.

However, keeping in mind that constitutionalism is a forward-oriented process, and assuming that the EU will survive the present crisis, the issue which remains open is whether the future efforts to eliminate the defects of the EU Constitution should be tied to traditional ways of thinking about democratic accountability within nation states, or we should stop thinking in terms of a Westphalian state, and accept that transnational systems can provide a cure for democratic failings in ways that differ from traditional postulates of direct majoritarian democracy.[90] This is, however, an issue for a different discussion.

---

89 Post, R. and Siegel, R., "Democratic Constitutionalism", in *The Constitution in 2020*, Balkin, J. and Siegel, R. (eds.), Oxford, Oxford University Press, 2009, p. 27.

90 For some hints see Moravcsik, A., *op. cit.*

Constitutional Identity of the European Union

Nenad DIMITRIJEVIĆ

Introduction

The European Union is in economic, political, and normative crisis. The crisis cannot be handled by ad hoc bureaucratic measures. It requires addressing anew the Union's fundamental questions. This paper focuses on the justification of the reasons for the Union's existence. The question is addressed in the identity perspective: who are "we the Europeans"; why are we together; what are the legitimate values and binding norms of our commonality?[1] I will argue that constitutional identity is a proper site for addressing these and related issues. The paper is divided in four sections. Section one outlines the contemporary European context and identifies different readings of European identity. Second two offers a short exposition of the concept of constitutional identity. Section three focuses on the Union. The emphasis is on an important controversial aspect of the Union's constitutionalism: the identity-specific relationship between historical particularity and constitutional universalism. Section four summarizes the main points by sketching an argument in favour of a European constitution.

1. What is European Identity?

In the very beginning I would like to claim the importance of an insight that might be bordering at obvious and trivial. The establishment of what we know today as the European Union (hereafter: the EU), was a matter of political choice; the capacity to choose what the Union is has remained one of its most striking features. In 1951, a group of the European leaders decided to side-step democracy and focus on coal and steel.[2] They did so in order to promote certain values; in their view, those values carried the

[1] For the brevity sake alone, this author – a European who is not a citizen of the Union – will use the pronoun "we" in the rest of this paper.

[2] Treaty Establishing the European Coal and Steel Community, 1951, at: http://europa.eu/legislation_summaries/institutional_affairs/treaties_ecsc_en.htm.

moral and civilizational weight beyond the democratic ayes and nays. Back to the present: on March 7, 2013 the Council of the EU postponed until the end of the year the decision of the expansion of the Schengen area to Romania and Bulgaria.[3] German Home Affairs Minister Hans-Peter Friedrich said in an interview that the crisis increased the risk of an influx into Germany of poor workers seeking social benefits. A new term – "benefits tourism" – was coined, and Great Britain, Austria, and the Netherlands joined Germany in denouncing this apparent, and apparently non-European, practice.[4]

Perhaps the latter choice bears some semblance of procedural legitimacy, but one thing is for sure: no trace of legitimate values can be identified in this decision. This is only one illustration of the current European crisis. The crisis is economic, political, and normative. The situation almost resembles a pre-revolutionary condition. The system seems not to be capable of responding to challenges: its measures cannot meet the requirements of efficacy, consistency, and procedural transparency. The actions of the Union's authorities cannot be seen as principled or right in a normative perspective either. The executives of the most powerful countries have adopted what has been identified as "ad hoc crisis management strategies" in the manner of "informal libertarian supranationalism".[5] It looks as if we are witnessing steps towards a perverted realisation of the cherished ideal of an "ever closer Union", with wrong actors who act in the wrong way, guided by the wrong goals, and causing bad consequences.

It seems that some basic questions about the EU have to be re-opened. What kind of entity is the Union? What are its fundamental values? What is, or what should be, in its substantive focus: handling of the systemic imperatives imposed by the increasing globalization, common economy, political integration, free movement of people, more effective protection of basic rights, peace, social solidarity, justice? If some combination of those or some other features is recognised as the Union's normative core, how it can be made to work harmoniously? How should legal and

---

3 Council of the European Union, Press Release, 3228th Council Meeting, Brussels, March 7-8 2013, at: http://www.consilium.europa.eu/Newsroom.

4 Nathalie Vandystadt, "Schengen: Sofia and Bucharest Forced to Wait Until End of Year", Europolitics, March 7 2013, at: http://europolitics.eis-vt-prod-web01.cyberadm.net/sectoral-policies/schengen-sofia-and-bucharest-forced-to-wait-until-end-of-year-art349043-16.html.

5 See for instance the critical articles collected by Eurozine, under the common title "The EU: Broken or Just Broke": Auer, Stefan, "The End of the European Dream"; Torreblanca, Jose Ignacio, "Five Reasons why Europe is Cracking Up"; Calliess, Christian, *et al.*, "Europe and the New German Question", at: http://www.eurozine.com/comp/focalpoints/eurocrisis.html.

political regime look like? Can there be a better democracy for the EU? Is democracy necessary for the EU? Is the democratic EU desirable at all? Is democracy possible in the EU? And how about constitution? Shall we stay content with the existing constitutional arrangement based on an uncodified set of Treaties, or would it still matter to have an act named constitution, and equipped not only with the requisite validity, but also with that special symbolic, legitimising and integrative authority of the words we usually associate with this act? Why not see the present crisis as the window of constitutional opportunity, go back to the drawing board, design democratic and inclusive constitution-making procedure, and make a full-fledged constitution?

Finally, the question that is in the focus of this paper asks: why are we together? Why have we chosen to create, or join, the Union? This is an identity question. The identity question of a political community is the question of what is common to its members. If the common core is missing, there is no community. What remains is rather through coercive means stabilised status of those who live, or who are forced to live, within given borders.[6] But how to define the common, that one that possibly links individuals and groups who either contingently happen to, or who decide to, live together? Broadly speaking, there exist several options. First, we can take a substantive view of identity, focusing for instance on the historically created, tradition-mediated, allegedly unrepeatable ethical commonality of "our nation", "our society", "our group-specific culture", and the like. Below I will try to show that, perhaps contrary to some intuitions, this perception of identity is not entirely alien to the Union. Second, our substantive focus can be on a present- and future-oriented common definition of the set of strategic rational reasons for being together. In the Union's case, this would amount to instrumental (mostly economic, but also security-specific) rationality as the primary cause for its establishment and preservation. Third, our shared identity can be shaped and expressed legally: member states, citizens, their relationships, institutions and their competencies, or rights, are all legal categories. The law defines the substance and creates the procedural framework of our selfhood; to identify us as "Europeans" means to identify our legal status. Fourth, our commonality can be based on the context-specific reading of moral universals. Of course, no political community rests on an unmediated application of moral values; they have to be translated into legal and political arrangements – this is where constitution enters.

6 Puhovski, Žarko, *Interes i zajednica* [*Interests and Community*], Zagreb, Liber, 1975, pp. 9-10.

In the following, I will defend the fourth reading of the European identity, arguing that it provides the most appropriate perspective of commonality for the Union and its multiple actors. The primacy of this approach does not imply its exclusivity. Shaping the Union's constitutional identity requires taking into account and finding a proper conceptual place for other three varieties of identity.

While the questions relevant for the analysis of constitutional identity are analytically separable, responses tend to overlap. Thus, my attempt at addressing the issues identified below will point rather to their interplay than to clear-cut answers to each of them. The proposed list of the questions is certainly not exhaustive. First, what is constitutional identity? Second, how it relates to pre-political identities? Does it presuppose a cultural homogeneity of a sort, or is it a matter of construction in a community that has some identifiable legal constitution? This also reads as the question of the source and conceptual place of constitutional identity. Third, what are the features of constitutional identity: which values and principles; which procedures, if any; which, if any, elements of the institutional set-up? Fourth, why constitutional identity matters, especially how it relates to democracy and its legitimacy? Fifth question concerns agency: who is, or who are, the bearers of this identity?

2. The Concept of Constitutional Identity

The concept of identity refers to the sense of selfhood of a person, group, or community across time and through different changes.[7] Identity lives in a tension between identifiability of *one as one*, on the one hand, and dynamism, on the other hand. To say that identity never implies statically perceived sameness, does not suggest the impossibility of saying the following: I was yesterday, and I am today, and I /hopefully/ will be tomorrow. The same holds for intergenerational non-voluntary groups, societies, or political communities. First, they are importantly constituted by their pasts, and by the manner of the past's appropriation through the practice of self-reflection. Second, self-reflection also looks forward, by identifying shared goals, interests, values, and their institutional formalization. In defining and re-defining the meaning of I or We along the past-present-future axis, we acknowledge the normative quality of dynamically understood shared selfhood.

Of course, much more can be, or has been, said. For instance, we can claim that identity is about existentially grounded authenticity.[8] We

7 Booth, W. James, "Communities of Memory: On Identity, Memory, and Debt", in *American Political Science Review*, Vol. 93, No. 2, 1999, p. 251.

8 Anthony Appiah, *The Ethics of Identity*, Princeton, Princeton University Press, 2005.

can agree that there cannot be identity without a certain minimum degree of homogeneity. We can proceed by asking if homogeneity of collective identity leaves room for internal pluralism. In response, we could follow communitarian argument that the internal complexity of collective identity – while requiring that we all be for "one", and while seeing this "one" as broadly socially given – still presupposes its dialogical, or relational quality.[9] Not least important, many people would insist that every identity assumes the figure of the "other".[10] A developed theory will perhaps argue that identity is a complex category, being at the same time existential and relational, objective and interpretative.[11] The question remains how to understand each of these qualities, and how to make sense of their relationship. A systematic study of these and related queries would require confronting different authors and theories. While avoiding this, I will later turn to some of these issues.[12]

How to discover constitutional identity?[13] I propose to understand this category as a particular aspect of the communal identity: it is the identity of a political community (and of its members), as shaped by valid, legitimate, and effective constitution. In some more detail, following Wojciech Sadurski, constitutional identity is "the set of values, principles and guidelines which define [...] the actually observed and enforced constraints within which day-to-day politics must take place."[14] This definition brings together values, procedures, and constraints: constitutional identity refers to common values and normative standards, the way they

9 Charles Taylor, *The Ethics of Authenticity*, Cambridge, MA, Harvard University Press, 1992.

10 The literature here becomes enormous, and I will just mention some of the relevant names: Georg Wilhelm Friedrich Hegel, Emmanuel Levinas, Jacques Derrida, Jean François Lyotard, Judith Butler, Edward Said, Miroslav Volf.

11 I borrow this particular emphasis on the complexity of identity from Vujadinović, Dragica, "Evropski politički identitet i Srbija" [European Political Identity and Serbia], in Podunavac, Milan, (ed.), *Ustav i demokratija u procesu transformacije* [*Constitution and Identity in the Processes of Transformation*], Belgrade, Fakultet političkih nauka, 2011, p. 45.

12 For a summary reading of how the theoretical controversies over the meaning of identity can be applied in the Union's context, see: Delanty, Gerard, "The Quest for European Identity", in Eriksen, Erik (ed.), *Making the European Polity. Reflexive Integration in the EU*, New York, Routledge, 2005, p. 129; Franzius, Claudio und Preuß, Ulrich, *Die Zukunft der europäischen Demokratie*, Berlin, Heinrich-Böll-Stiftung, 2012, p. 37.

13 The literature on constitutional identity is rich. For especially valuable contributions, see Jacobsohn, Gary, *Constitutional Identity*, Cambridge, MA, Harvard University Press, 2010; Rosenfeld, Michel, *The Identity of the Constitutional Subject: Selfhood, Citizenship, Culture, and Community*, New York, Routledge, 2009.

14 Sadurski, Wojciech, "European Constitutional Identity?", in *EUI Working Paper in Law*, No. 33, 2006, p. 1.

are formalised in the constitution, and applied in the political and social processes of a community.

This brings back the categories of selfhood, dynamism, and interpretation. How do they apply to constitutional identity? Interpretation concerns assigning the dominant, or right, or legally binding meaning to the constitutional values, words, and practices. It first applies to the constitutional choice at the moment of foundation. The authors of the first constitution are often called "Founders", because the very establishment of the community and its institutional form result from their decision. History of constitution making shows that this choice is preceded by an interpretation of the past, reflection on the present condition, and identification of the goals for the future. These interpretations and the constitutive decision can be right or wrong. My claim is not that the fate of a polity is determined by the original choice – it is only that the importance of that choice cannot be disregarded.

Second, interpretation points that we are never simply caught into a normative, substantive and institutional-procedural framework as it had been envisaged and set up by the Founders. Individual and collective selfhood are to an important extent matters of broadly understood time-specific and context-specific constitutional interpretation.[15] The term "broadly understood" implies that this interpretation includes virtually all actions in the constitutionally shaped field, by any actor, from an individual right holder to legislature. Or, we can talk about a "constitutionally relevant interpretation". It points to social, political and legal actions and practices that agents, addressees, and observers alike identify as constitutional, or constitution-specific. Constitutionally relevant interpretation is the process in which we discover the meaning of the terms like "authoritative", 'allowed', "forbidden", "right", or "wrong". It is based on, derived from, and justified by constitutional norms and the past constitutional practices. For instance, when a New Yorker David reflects on whether the free speech clause of the US Constitution allows him to criticize the government or express his views on the Tea Party, he invokes both his interpretation of his own constitutional identity (David the American citizen), and of the constitutional identity of the political community: his country – the US – would not be what it is if it did not allow for a free expression of opinions in controversial matters of public concern. When a Bulgarian citizen protests against the recent Schengen decision, she raises the claim that this particular constraint denies her equality with other European citizens, thus challenging her constitutionally guaranteed identity. Second,

15 See Mahlmann, Mathias, "Constitutional Identity and the Politics of Homogeneity", in *German Law Review*, Vol. 6, No. 2, 2005, p. 308.

she can also argue that this decision affects the constitutional identity of the EU itself, undermining its legitimacy; the decision denies the application of one of the EU's founding principles – free movement of people – to one particular, substantively singled out group of its citizens (substantive criterion being "benefits tourism").

In short, we expect constitutional identity to be the normative framework that legitimately harmonizes our particular identities, different worldviews, and plurality of our self-interests. This term combines legal validity and substantive commitments to summarise – in a fashion stable, binding, transparent, and legitimate – something that is common to all of us. We believe that that something is worthy of being formalised in the constitution, and given special protection. Formalisation and protection of values and standards in constitutional norms and practices do not imply that these values and standards are exempted from discussion or even conflict. But the assumption is that the discussion is constrained to the question of their true meaning. Another assumption is that this identity is authoritative, in at least two senses: first, pluralism of values and standards is reduced to those values and standards that are constitutionally recognised; second, their true meaning in the pluralist condition will be ultimately established by constitutional judiciary, as the agency equipped with the authority to inform us about the binding reading of constitution.

What is the content of constitutional identity? In constitutional democracies, it is composed of the principles of individual autonomy, equal liberty for all members of the polity, tolerance and pluralism, human dignity and social justice, which in a communal perspective become principles of the government-specific duties of equal care and equal concern. The institutionalisation of these principles is also well known: basic rights, popular sovereignty, the rule of law, separation of powers, limited government, special protection of structural minorities, and – in social liberal reading – policies of re-distribution aimed at fighting social inequalities for the sake of preserving equal opportunities as a necessary background of a meaningful idea of autonomy.

Of course, problems and controversies are many. Take the following well-known issue. Democratic political process is not only about free discussion under the condition of the procedurally guaranteed equality of our particular perspectives. It is also about cutting deliberation short by producing binding decisions. Such decisions will know of winners and losers. How to justify this particular coercive limitation of our original freedom and equality? One response points to democracy as self-rule. While being admittedly the central part of the answer, it does not suffice, because the very concept of democracy carries a coercion-specific paradox: by participating in making, or by agreeing to, a law, I become the co-author not only of the coercion applied against me; I also co-authorize coercion against others.[16] What gives me the right to authorize the coercion against others? And against which others?

The classical liberal response derives democracy from the claim of the conceptual primacy of the individual perspective. The positive core of the constitutional identity applies to all, and no defeat in any discrete political competition should ever challenge this. When the Tea Party wins the elections, David the Opponent remains the holder of all the constitutionally guaranteed rights. His rights-mediated constitutional identity is beyond the political competition because it protects his moral identity of a human being equal to others. This is one of the principal criteria of legitimacy of a constitutional order: main features of constitutional identity are protected against democratic majority rule. This supposedly also helps managing the question we find on the flip side of the legitimacy coin – that of political obligation. Our (assumed, but only conditional) duty to obey is partly derived from our political loyalty shaped by our constitutional identity. The claim is that in democracy both majority and minority are the people. Citizenry is composed of members who are safely fluctuating between majorities and minorities, never really losing the core of their identity and constitutional status.

Still, there seems to be something circular, or perhaps missing, in this reasoning. Here is a sceptical question: how can you expect the citizens to agree on the special status of constitutional essentials, leaving only the rest for a pluralist competition? The answer "because they are the constitutional *demos*" does not really work, claims the sceptic. We cannot simply assume that citizenry of a polity is a constitutional construct. The very idea and realistic possibility of obedience are to an important extent informed by the logic of the original constitutional choice. The question is: where does the identification of the peoplehood come from? Who and how decides who the people are, and how this original choice affects democratic legitimacy?

The search for a response seems to bring us closer to a social thesis of a sort. Constitution-makers have to explain what exactly defines this particular community, what distinguishes it from others, why is this particular set of moral universalist claims translated into this particular legal-constitutional language, and why is it valid for all of us, being at same time exclusively valid only for us who live within these borders? The answer to the question of who is "we" cannot be invented at will. Political rule is unpleasant because its coercive character holds a great

16 Michelman, Frank, "Constitutional Authorship", in Alexander, Larry (ed.), *Constitutionalism. Philosophical Foundations*, Cambridge, MA, Cambridge University Press, 1998, p. 82.

potential for injustice. To endure it without feeling merely oppressed, we need some "cement of society"[17] beyond the constitutional proclamation of moral universals. Political identity presupposes social embeddedness. Put simply, on this reading, majority rule requires a clearly socialized sense of political identity: it requires a sound cultural background.

3. Constitutional Identity of the Union: Towards a Context-Specific Universalism

The approach based on the social thesis weighs heavily in the context of the EU democracy discussion. Authors like Peter Graf Kielmansegg and Dieter Grimm argue that the EU is missing on this embeddedness.[18] This also reads as the absence of the common good and solidarity. It follows that the Union lacks the underlying commonality that would make majority rule legitimately possible. A paradoxical situation follows, in which so many are unhappy with the democratic deficit, while at the same time many seem to realise that a classical version of representative democracy would lead to the domination of the more powerful states. Representative democracy with its majoritarian institutions is perceived as a threat to cultural and political identities of the member states.[19]

There are several ways to respond to this challenge. First strategy argues that the EU is not a proper site for democracy, re-affirming the stance that has been lingering around from the very beginning: the intergovernmental functionalist approach that understands the Union as the community of sovereign states bound together by a series of contracts. Second strategy proposes to resort to a consensus-oriented institutional arrangement among member states as the thick identity-holders, adding the EU citizenship to the equation, which would amount to the picture of the EU federalism. Third strategy advocates a consensus-oriented reasoned deliberation in the condition of constitutionally recognized deep diversity.

17 I borrow this phrase from Jon Elster, who gives it a different meaning. Elster, Jon, *The Cement of Society. A Study of Social Order*, Cambridge, Cambridge University Press, 1989.

18 Graf von Kielmansegg, Peter, "Integration und Demokratie", in Jachtenfuchs, Markus, Kohler-Koch, Beate (eds.), *Europäische Integration*, Stuttgart, UTB, 2003; here after Kaina, Viktoria and Karolewski, Ireneusz, "EU Governance and European Identity", in *Living Reviews in European Governance*, Vol. 4, No. 2, 2009, pp. 8-9. See also Grimm, Dieter, "Integration by Constitution", I-CON, Vol. 3, No. 2-3, 2005, p. 198; Grimm, Dieter, *Die Zukunft der Verfassung II: Auswirkungen von Europäisierung und Globalisierung*, Berlin, Suhrkamp, 2012, pp. 92, 212, 275.

19 Eriksen, Erik, "European Transformation. A Pragmatic Approach", in ARENA Working Paper, No. 7, 2010, pp. 6-8, at: http://www.arena.uio.no.

"Depth" of diversity points to what is presented as both the empirical strength and the inescapable conceptual relevance of national cultures and political identities of the member states: deep diversity stands for "persistent pluralism". The hope is that deliberative practices would open up the thick identities in direction of creating a thin but constitutionally operational Union-specific sense of selfhood and belonging.[20] The list of options does not end here. For instance, it is unclear whether deep diversity has to remain the building block of a thin European identity. Habermas' most recent reading of the EU-specific cosmopolitanism apparently does not rely conceptually on deep diversity. I will be back to this.

We encounter here a difficult question of the relationship between constitutional universals and a particular historical context. The question is legitimate.[21] Still, perhaps there is a difference between acknowledging the constitutional relevance of a state's history, cultural and political traditions, on the one hand, and accepting history and traditions as the basis of the constitutional formulation of demos and political community, on the other hand. Consider Habermas' methodological guidance:

> Even if such a community is grounded in the universalist principles of a democratic constitutional state, it still forms a collective identity, in the sense that it interprets and realizes these principles in light of its own history and in the context of its own political form of life.[22]

In search for a normatively right and institutionally feasible way of managing this tension, it is important to identify and preserve the conceptual distinction between cultural and constitutional identities. These two categories are not derived one from another. Rather, at stake is a complex interplay. This interplay indeed depends on the historical and cultural context, but the dependence does not, or should not, read as the primacy of particular ethical situated givens over morally founded constitutional universalism.[23] It is

---

20 Compare a summary account on how the three models of integration proposed by RECON (Reconstituting Democracy in Europe project) reflect on the European identity, in Góra, Magdalena and Mach, Zdzisław, "Identity Formation, Democracy and European Integration", in Góra, Magdalena and Mach, Zdzisław (eds.), *Collective Identity and Democracy. The Impact of EU Enlargement*, RECON Report Series, Arena, Oslo, 2010, pp. 15 et passim, at: http://www.reconproject.eu.

21 Those who think that the question is not legitimate are few. For a radical universalist position on the EU identity that challenges the relevance of cultural identities of member states, see Mahlmann, *op. cit.*, p. 312.

22 Habermas, Jürgen, *Postnational Constellation. Political Essays*, Cambridge, Polity Press, 2001, p. 107.

23 In this paper the terms "ethics" and "morality" are used to distinguish between the group-specific concept of the good life (ethics) and universal normative standards of right (morality).

perhaps safe to argue that the two types of identity have to be in some kind of harmony. However, this harmony is not delivered by our history. It is something to be achieved; the question is how exactly in the given context constitutional universalism will be formulated, interpreted and applied.

Let us recall bits of history of modern constitutionalism. One relevant lesson is that for a political community the question of legitimate combination of the group-specific ethics and moral universals comes down to identifying not merely the integrative capacity and the feasibility of each, but also – and centrally – the legitimate constitutional-democratic place of each. Since the French revolution *demos* is a constitutional category. The French case also shows that constitutional identities of the people and political community are not necessarily rubber stumps on the cultural given: the constitution does not have to reflect the dominant culture. Also, the Germany after World War II and the post-apartheid South Africa demonstrate, albeit in different ways, that we can – sometimes we even have to – build political community and civic solidarity by openly confronting the dominant culture.[24]

Another important lesson follows: social homogeneity, trust and solidarity, while they in some historical cases do precede constitutional design, are not conceptual preconditions of constitutional democracy. These important identity features are always to some extent tasks. Sometimes, however, they are tasks very difficult to fulfil, due to the lack of societal cohesion or solidarity, prevailing mistrust, or even a condition in which basic moral distinctions between right and wrong are heavily challenged. Sometimes societies find themselves in the moral, cultural, and political ruins. Amid the legacies of disaster they have to ask what it means to build a decent society and polity. In such situations constitution is introduced as a blueprint of a desired novelty, which has little or no cultural backing. Constitutional identity – from values to institutional arrangements – becomes the image of what we think how we ought to be. Constitutional design conflates with normative constructivism. Did this turn Germany of 1949 and afterwards, or South Africa of 1993 and afterwards, into the constitutional constructs without foundations? The answer is negative: given that constitutional designers departed from the insight into the social constraints of the founding moment, the respective constitutions cannot be rejected as cases of voluntaristic constructivism. The formal-constitutional response to the challenge of the foundational moment assumed the form of the reflective attitudes to the recent past. Having reflected on the

24 Compare Robert Goodin's instructive discussion on "moral desiderata": Goodin, Robert, "Institutions and Their Design", in Goodin, Robert (ed.), *The Theory of Institutional Design*, Cambridge, Cambridge University Press, 1996, p. 37.

deficit of legacies of democratic constitutionalist political culture, or on a particularly sinister past that left a cultural legacy of moral corruption, or on some combination of those, constitution-makers chose to construct a radical constitutional alternative. They resorted to an authoritative reading that distinguished between legitimate and non-legitimate features in their inherited collective identities.

It follows that the popular phrase "community of fate" can point to different kinds of fates. By now the direction of my argument may be plain: the EU is not an abstract universalist construct. It is both empirically and normatively inaccurate to argue that a constitutional project for a more democratic and more integrated Union is neither feasible nor legitimate due to the deficit of the European cultural identity. The EU is a "community of fate". Its democratic-constitutional question is not how to proceed from the allegedly unquestionable, constitutionally mediated group-specific ethics that member states bring as a bride price to that moral universalist but allegedly "bloodless" entity that would be the EU. The question is how to make sense of Europe's existential ground, which is both positive and negative. Recall Habermas and Derrida's 2003 declaration: European identity combines "the consciousness of a shared political fate and the prospect of a common future."[25] The EU was conceived

25 Habermas, Jürgen and Derrida, Jacques, "February 15, or What Binds Europeans Together: A Plea for a Common Foreign Policy, Beginning in the Core of Europe", in *Constellations*, Vol. 10, No. 3, 2003, p. 293. Given that in this text I refer to Habermas a lot, it deserves to be mentioned that this declaration is the place where he for the first time announced a concept I find highly contestable – that of the "core Europe". In his most recent book on Europe – *The Crisis of the European Union. A Response*, Cambridge, Polity Press, 2012 – and in numerous recent short texts and interviews, Habermas insists on the differentiation of the EU into a core and a periphery. Europe has been badly affected by the recent devastating bureaucratic efforts to save Euro – these efforts only further destroy trust and solidarity as the necessary fundamental values of the Union. In response, the core Europe should be identified and formally established: it would be composed of the members of the Euro zone, where the monetary union would be expanded into a core Political Union. Habermas apparently believes that these countries carry the greatest responsibility for the Union as a "community of fate". He argues that this responsibility within the new core Union would be met by overcoming the current concept of sovereignty, which still relies on the member states as the sovereign subjects of the treaties. In its stead would come a true popular sovereignty of the citizens of the core Union, the normative basis and institutional architecture of which would focus of overcoming the chronic democratic deficit of the EU. The old intergovernmentalism would be finally abandoned in favour of a democratically legitimized core Union. Through a series of proposed institutional innovations, the core Union would become a proper site of the "democratic will formation", meaning that the citizens would cease to see it as an alienated power centre that trumps their democratic self-rule shaped at the member state levels. This "democracy in the core", based on shared (citizens' and peoples') popular sovereignty, would be both post-national and cosmopolitan. Cosmopolitanism would rely on Europe-specific

against the background of interplay of two sets of legacies. On the one side is the reaffirmation of a string of positive, living, though highly vulnerable traditions, ranging from the Enlightenment to social rights. On the other side, the European cultural and political project emerged in direct opposition to the dominant culture of fear, mistrust, rivalry, and even hatred in the wake of the World War II.[26] Sure, such positive and negative identity features are not exclusively European. Still, the way of their experience and appropriation is distinctly European. Hence we can safely consider them the points of the EU identity. The relational features of the Union's identity follow from thus understood normative reading of its existential ground. The European project is about pluralism of cultures and democracies most of whom have experienced series of cultural and moral failures prior to joining the Union. The Union brings together, protects, and promotes the pluralism of life-worlds, each of which has shaped its constitutional regime on reflection about the past.

The original result of this reflection, and the founding act of the European constitutionalism, was the Schuman Declaration. Its normative basis is unequivocal: "The contribution which an organized and living Europe can bring to civilization is indispensable to the maintenance of peaceful relations."[27] The message, even if implied, is clear enough. It tells

---

reading of constitutional patriotism, rather than on an abstract Kantian moral universalism. The old state sovereignty would remain with "periphery states": no change in the constitutional treaties of the EU will be possible without their consent (see in particular "Democracy, Solidarity and the European Crisis", Lecture delivered by Jürgen Habermas on 26 April 2013 in Leuven, at:http://www.kuleuven.be/communicatie/evenementen/evenementen/jurgen-habermas/democracy-solidarity-and-the-european-crisis). Habermas believes that this proposal also reflects a reality in which some of the Central-East European member states and Great Britain are reluctant to hand over important features of their sovereignty to a supranational union. However, it remains largely unclear how the relationship between the core and the periphery would look like. The claim that belonging to the Euro zone deepens the members' responsibilities, which can be handled only in a genuine post-national, post-statist, and cosmopolitan way, is already in itself legally and politically controversial. But leaving the "periphery states" largely out of analytical focus simply means failing to address the core questions of the character of the EU as a whole: two types of orders would exist within the EU, with two sets of legal norms and institutional arrangements, based on different normative standards. Taken together, such differences would likely undermine the core principles of Habermas' project: democratic self-rule, "civilization of state power", trust, solidarity, and equality.

26 This is of course a point shared by many authors. For more recent renderings see e.g. Beck, Ulrich, *Das Deutsche Europa. Neue Machtlandschaften im Zeichen der Krise*, Suhrkamp, Berlin, 2012, p. 12; Leggewie, Claus, *Der Kampf um die europäische Erinnerung. Ein Schlachtfeld wird besichtigt*, München, C.H. Beck, 2011, pp. 7-45.

27 The Schuman Declaration, 1950, at: http://europa.eu/about-eu/basic-information/symbols/europe-day/schuman-declaration/index_en.htm.

us that after the totalitarian and authoritarian experiences of the 20th century, after the Holocaust, Gulag and Srebrenica, no attempt to close the books and simply re-instate our "true traditions" and positive moral, legal and political legacies, can stand the test of justification. Civilization requires peace, and peace cannot be built and preserved on forgetting. In this context, the strange foundational focus on coal and steel becomes clear, at least at a symbolic level: "The pooling of coal and steel production […] will change the destinies of those regions which have long been devoted to the manufacture of munitions of war, of which they have been the most constant victims."[28] The Schuman Declaration reads that we have joined together because only united we can change the course of our shared history. Europe never missed on commonality, but only with the original establishment of the European Communities a principled attempt was made not to base this commonality on accident and force. It is only through reflection on its negative legacies that Europe can re-affirm its valuable traditions in the present and future. This shared insight – rather than recognition of "deep diversity" among the multitude of member states – provides the basis of European pluralism.

However, there are different objections to the constitutional relevance of thus understood European pluralist culture.

One objection says that member states, each on its own, have demonstrated their capacities to learn from their pasts. Germany has built a respectable democracy. France called for a European peace and solidarity to be lead by Franco-German reconciliation back in the late 1940s, when it was easier to remain cynical and suspicious. The post-communist countries fought their own, mostly nationalistic, demons when choosing the constitutional democratic and European paths after the decades of authoritarianism. Simply put, cultural identities of member states have already been constitutionalized. Europe consists of 28 democracies: interplay between culture and statehood has been established 28 times in the form of constitutional identity. The normative claim then reads that "we the people" already live under the regimes of constitutional democracy, exercising legitimate liberal-democratic self-rule in our context-specific ways. Then why do we need the Union at all, if the "persistent pluralism" of our ethical conceptions of the good finds its more "spontaneous" expression in our national communities? If at the level of member states we have fewer problems with being together, then apparently this safe haven is, or should be, also a safer place than the EU to defend rights, democracy and the rule of law in times of crisis.

---

[28] *Ibid.*

A related objection argues that "learning from disaster" approach is used up. Recall Joseph Weiler's famous summary of the three original reasons for a new Europe after the World War II: ensuring peace, promoting prosperity, and overcoming discrimination on grounds of nationality.[29] However, to use the phrase of the same author, this "political messianism"[30] has had its day, meaning simply that it cannot serve as a normative basis of the processes of integration anymore. At one point even Habermas, the staunchest proponent of "learning from disaster" as a necessary feature of the European political culture, seemed to agree.[31] Still, it may not be obvious how we could leave behind the sinister aspects of the European 20th century. It is not obvious either that we can trust the member states in their discrete processes of appropriating the difficult episodes of their histories. Rather than seeing it as "political messianism", I believe that the claim of the relevance of the past as a shared past is a sober analytical extrapolation from the age of disasters. At stake is the past that we should not allow to pass, the past that ought to remain as a moral yardstick for the contemporary generations as well. Today, when the crisis keeps bringing old and new stereotypes, from "the southern laziness" to the posters of Angela Merkel with Hitler-like moustaches, the Union should insist on remembering the tenor of the Schuman Declaration: "[…] Peace cannot be safeguarded without the making of creative efforts proportionate to the dangers which threaten it."[32]

Sure, the claim of the presence of the memory in the political constitution of contemporary Europe is a normative consideration rather than an empirical fact. One can always say that all those prejudices and retrograde movements we have witnessed recently are not really causally linked to the worst European episodes, or that they are not really explicable in terms of some undesirable re-appropriation of the political and cultural memories. But the point is exactly that you can

29 Weiler, Joseph, *The Constitution of Europe*, Cambridge, Cambridge University Press, 1999, here after Joerges, Christian, "Working Through 'Bitter Experiences' Towards a Purified European Identity? A Critique of the Disregard for History in European Constitutional Theory and Practice", in Eriksen, Erik, Joerges, Christian and Rödl, Florian (eds.), *Law, Democracy and Solidarity in a Post-National Union. The Unsettled Political Order of Europe*, London, Routledge, 2008, p. 179.

30 Weiler, Joseph, "The Political and Legal Culture of European Integration: An Exploratory Essay", I-CON, Vol. 9, No. 3-4, 2011, p. 682; Weiler, Joseph, "60 Years since the First European Community – Reflections on Political Messianism", in *European Journal of International Law*, Vol. 22, No. 2, 2011, at: http://www.ejiltalk.org/60-years-since-the-first-european-community-%E2%80%93-reflections-on-political-messianism/.

31 Habermas, Jürgen, "Why Europe Needs a Constitution", in *New Left Review*, 11/2001, 7.

32 *The Schuman Declaration, op. cit.*

see them both ways: the question is not what they empirically are, but how we choose to interpret them, in light of the empirically observable crisis. How shall Germans think and act in response to the crisis that keeps devastating some of its fellow EU member states? How shall Greeks respond to the Nazi moniker stamped on the current German government?

Recall another slogan from Habermas' and Derrida's declaration: "It's easy to find unity without commitment."[33] To commit to Europe today means to abandon as illegitimate the practices that toy with political arrogance and cynicism of power, especially those based on the logic of economic strength winning over those economically weak. Greater economic power should not translate into greater political authority. If this is not appreciated, and if the trend in which economically powerful dictate the political shape of Europe, its landscape of rights, the reach of social, legal and political equality of its citizens, and the worth of this or that member state, is not reversed very soon, Europe will continue sliding into the abyss, becoming more and more a kind of Leviathan that understands and exercises the power as the "absence of external impediments of motion."[34] Further, to commit to Europe means confronting those who toy with Nazi or fascist symbols, not because such a confrontation would be politically correct, but because after the whole European devastating experience with racism and extreme nationalism, using Nazism as a metaphor when criticizing opponents, or when attacking those whose positions one finds repugnant, falls way below basic standards of human decency. Also, to commit means to argue that Europe has arrived to the point where we have to understand and accept that economic problems in one of its parts or social suffering of some of its citizens, are matters of concern for all. Identity-wise, there can be no Europe without shared sensibilities and solidarity.

4. On Importance of Making the Right Choice

Shortly, in negative terms, Europe requires refraining from certain attitudes, beliefs, and practices. Only with such self-restraints entrenched, it becomes possible to defend and affirm the European common core, which I propose to see as a sense of shared responsibility focused on a set of requirements on what we owe to each other: trust, solidarity, equal freedom, respect for diversity, and justice. This combination of negative and positive elements of substantive identity provides the basis of the Union's constitutional identity. Each of these elements can be found explicated

33 Derrida, Jacques and Habermas, Jürgen, *op. cit.*, p. 293.

34 Hobbes, Thomas, *Leviathan*, Chapters XIV, XXI, different editions.

in different legal acts that together make up for the Union's constitution, and it provides the basis for what I identified above as a constitutionally relevant interpretation. Or, if we see Europe as a normative project legitimacy and feasibility of which depend on the constitutional appropriation of interplay between positive and negative identity features, we can perhaps talk about the constituent interpretation, based on the reflectively appropriated duty to make the right choice.

The argument that positive features of the Union's constitutional identity should be read in the context of Europe's negative experiences is not meant to deny that much has changed since the foundation. The Union has achieved a lot, advancing goods like peace, liberty, prosperity, and solidarity to the levels previously unknown in the history of the Continent. Let us also not forget that the Union has undergone successive waves of expansion. Each expansion meant much more than a mere physical enlargement: it brought new states, cultures, and human beings with their distinct communal, group-specific, and individual histories, cultures, experiences, normative standards, and expectations. In consequence, the life together in the Union has assumed a unique open-ended form, in which borders and membership are not settled. This uniqueness-in-dynamics had to be acknowledged through the adjustment or change in the legal-institutional framework and normative identity of the Union.[35] A lot has been done in this department too. But the present crisis warns that not enough has been done, or that something has been done wrongly. The gravity of today's stakes reduces and sharpens dramatically the range of available options.

The old instrumental, intergovernmental, and quasi constitutional model has been apparently exhausted. In a sense, the crisis has brought the Union back to the very beginning, posing again a question that the Founders had avoided: the question of democracy. This return of the democratic question has nothing to do with the so-called paradox of foundation, which would inform that no democracy can be established democratically. Besides, the Union has never been confronted with the mysterious constitutional meta-question of the constituent power.[36]

35 For a detailed analysis of the genealogy of the EU enlargement process, and its constitutional and normative implications, see e.g. Fossum, John Erik and Menendez, Agustin Jose, *Constitution's Gift. A Constitutional Theory for a Democratic European Union*, Lanham, Rowman & Littlefield, 2011, pp. 45 *et passim*.

36 I am aware that many authors would contest this claim. See e.g. Priban, Jiri, "The Juridification of European Identity, its Limitations and the Search of EU Democratic Politics", in *Constellations*, Vol. 16, No. 1, 2009, p. 44. A detailed defence of my claim would go beyond the scope of this paper, given that it would require an abstract theoretical analysis of the meaning of the constituent power, and, in particular, its

In 1951 it was technically possible to make a new organization democratically, given that the constitutions of the founding member states contained democratically legitimized integration mandates.[37] These mandates were used to establish the first move as legal, in a manner of constitutional continuity, allowing for the subsequent steps to unfold as "a process of integration through law."[38] But the democratic path was not chosen, leaving the room for the constituent power question to make a late entrance, in the form of the "no-demos" complaint. Recall that the Founders opted for the strategy that assigned the constitutionalist primacy of the constraining values over democratic will formation and decision-making: a new reading of the founding values of constitutionalism was offered in a manner both authoritative and non-democratic. This choice was amplified by not providing a blueprint for a possible future democracy either. Instead of a democratic roadmap, a blurry perception of dynamic, organic growth of democracy out of spirit of gradually increasing economic rationality was offered.

In short, even though the original values have retained their place, the instrumental logic of integration has proven increasingly obsolete. Integration and expansion have travelled from an economic cooperation to a multi-layered polity of today, bringing along the way an ever-broadening pluralism of the interpretations of the Union's normative core. While the extraordinarily dense history of the Union's constitutional and political reforms testifies to the awareness of the democracy question, the democratic quality of integration has remained under-developed, largely due to the persistent deep disagreement over the question of the legal and political character of the polity. Highly fashionable (and, admittedly, sometimes highly sophisticated) academic and policy discourses on "non-hierarchical", "diffused", "fragmented", "novel-in-kind", "*sui generis*", "beyond the state" European polity, routinely clash with equally fashionable complaints about the democratic deficit. These discourses apparently do not have the capacity to address the present crisis. Novelty that the EU has brought may be a fascinating thing; the problem, however, is that "we the Europeans" do not agree on what Europe is. This is perhaps best expressed in the paradoxes that surround the character of the EU law.[39] In spite of the best efforts of the European Court of Justice, and in spite of the – most of the time present – remarkable readiness of

---

relationship to the constitution-making power. This latter relationship concerns both agency and its relationship to law; it is often overlooked in theory, which somewhat routinely distinguishes only between the constituent and constituted powers.

37 Fossum, John Erik and Menendez, Agustin Jose, *Constitution's Gift*, *op. cit.*, pp. 36, 79.

38 *Ibid.*, p. 49.

39 *Ibid.*, p. 88.

member states to accept the authority of the Union's law, "[legal] practice is deeply muddled and lacks a clear, principled foundation, which cannot be forthcoming in the absence of a solution to the polity and legitimacy puzzles."[40] Given that there is no agreement on the character of the polity, it is small wonder that legitimacy gap is manifold and ever widening. Operating as informal and non-transparent management of the crisis of an entity whose institutional, legal, and normative coordinates are largely unknown, policies designed and applied today can hardly reflect legitimacy criteria of self-rule, transparency, rightness, solidarity, justice, efficacy, or adequacy.

At a general level, the response to the dilemmas of the Union's political quality, legitimacy, and validity of its legal system, may be deceptively simple. The Union needs an authoritative settlement of these big issues. In terms of the central concern of this paper, the EU requires establishing a unified, institutionally streamlined, and legally unambiguously binding constitutional regime. The regime would have to provide an authoritative answer to the question of the character of the polity by settling in constitutional terms the Union's identity as "centred on universalist liberal democratic values, refracted and interpreted through particular historical experiences and political cultures."[41]

This is the proposal for a European Constitution. The Union needs a codified, democratically prepared and enacted highest act. Let me repeat: the exhaustion of the old functionalist model, the continuous expansion of the Union, the erratic process of political institutionalization followed by the increasing problem of the democratic deficit, today's problems of economic crisis, political mismanagement, and the threat of social implosion, have all sharpened the problem of the Union's identity to the point at which it has to be either democratically restructured or abandoned altogether. Given that the path travelled thus far has been long and the changes it brought appear irreversible,[42] and given the seriousness of the current crisis, the situation presents itself as a constitutional moment. It is obvious that this claim raises many questions for democratic theory and practice: what would it mean to make a constitution in a democratic and inclusive manner; who would be the constitution-makers; how to organize a meaningful communication between the agents of a would-be European democracy (citizens, *demos*, "*demoi*", member states, political and social

---

40 *Ibid.*, p. 3.

41 Müller, Jan-Werner, "A 'Thick' Constitutional Patriotism for the EU? On Morality, Memory and Militancy", in Eriksen, Erik, Joerges, Christian and Rödl, Florian (eds.), *Law, Democracy and Solidarity in a Post-National Union*, *op. cit.*, pp. 30, 206.

42 Habermas, Jürgen, "Why Europe Needs a Constitution", *op. cit.*, pp. 32, 7.

organizations), and the constitution-making body; how, in accordance with which procedural rules, to make the highest act; what would be the content of such a constitution?[43] This paper stops short of addressing these and related issues, given that its task was only to offer reasons that justify a new beginning in democratic constitutionalism for Europe.

---

[43] "Introduction. A Constitution in the Making?" by Editors, in Eriksen, Erik, Fossum, John Erik and Menendez, Agustin Jose (eds.), *Developing a Constitution for Europe*, London, Routledge, 2005, pp. 1-3.

European Constitutional Patriotism

Dragica Vujadinović

Introduction

The background points of this analysis are: 1. The issue of political identity has been primarily related to the frame of the nation-state; 2. Each political identity has three mutually connected dimensions, firstly, an objective dimension (institutional and legal framework), secondly, a subjective dimension (sense of belonging, commitment to a political community), and thirdly, an interpretative dimension (political identity has never been a given, it is always a certain interpretation); 3. Elites create certain relevant interpretations of political identity, and that consequently leads to the responsibility of elites for a normative quality and political implications of those interpretations; 4. Identity of the nation-state, as the primary form of a modern polity, can be the subject of ethno-cultural and/or civic interpretation; 5. Constitutional patriotism – with its founding the commitment in universal values and constitutional principles – represents the civic version of interpreting the nation-state political identity; 6. Constitutional patriotism also represents the subjective dimension and is thus essentially linked to the institutional framework of constitutional democracy (the given objective dimension of political identity); 7. European Union (hereafter EU) represents the political community with a certain political identity, which overcomes the context and content of the nation-state; 8. Discourse on objective, subjective and interpretative dimensions of political identity, as well as the discussion of an ethno-cultural and civic interpretation of political identity is on the agenda also in the case of the EU; 9. All above-mentioned dimensions and interpretations have had specific features in the case of the EU, which represents a supranational political body with an open-ended building process; 10. European constitutional patriotism means a civic version of interpretation, which legitimizes the EU on the basis of institutionalized and legally formalized constitutional principles and values; 11. Constitutional patriotism fits essentially better than the ethno-cultural interpretation to the institutional and legal-political framework of the EU.

1. Constitutional Patriotism

The concept of constitutional patriotism originally relates to the concept of political identity of the nation state, being a democratic legal state and/or democratic constitutional state.[1]

Besides linking closely to the concept of political identity, the concept of constitutional patriotism is also connected with the concepts of political legitimacy, culture of human rights, democratic political culture, public space, constitutional culture, and constitutional identity.

Constitutional patriotism represents a normative civic *interpretation* of political identity, one based on universal values and human rights. When internalized by individual citizens it also becomes a version of the *subjective dimension* of political identity – a sense of belonging to the democratic constitutional state. It is inseparable from an institutional and legal-political structure of the modern constitutional state (the *objective dimension* of political identity).

Constitutional patriotism means a mode of attachment to the political body, which is very much different from pre-political ties to which the nation states have traditionally appealed.[2]

Although the civic interpretation of democratic legal/constitutional state best fits to its character, ethno-cultural interpretation of the liberal-democratic state is also possible; the accent in that case is on ethnic and cultural features of the given nation state instead of on its constitutional identity; contrary to that, constitutional patriotism presupposes a commitment to shared political principles and human rights protection rather than to shared ethno-national identities.

The concept emerged in post-World War II Germany. It achieved new popularity in the late 1990s, as it became an attractive model for explaining the legitimizing capacities of liberal democratic nation-states. It also started being used as a normative model for understanding European

---

* This article is a result of the work on the Project "Constitutionalism and Rule of Law in the Nation-State Building – the Case of Serbia", funded by the Ministry of Science of the Republic of Serbia.

1 Robert Alexy differentiates a "formal legal state", "democratic legal state", and "democratic constitutional state". (Alexy, R., "Die Institutionalisierung der Menschenrechte im demokratischen Verfassungsstaat", in Gosepath, S., Lohman, G. (Hg.), *Philosophie der Menschenrechte*, Frankfurt am Main, Suhrkamp Verlag, 2013, pp. 244-264).

2 Habermas, J., *The Inclusion of the Other*, Polity Press, Cambridge, Massachusetts, 1998. Also: Fossum, J.E., "On the Prospects for a Viable Constitutional Patriotism in Complex Multinational Entities: Canada and the European Union Compared", http://www.academia.edu/3029998/On_the_Prospects_for_a_Viable_Constitutional_Patriotism_in_Complex_Multinational_Entities_Canada_and_the_European_Union_Compared, p. 2.

identity as a supranational political community. A part of the reason for this new popularity is related to its capacity for matching the requirements of the rising trends of multiculturalism in the age of globalization, in both nation states and the EU.

Sternberger introduced this concept in 1979 (and even before, in 1958). His attempt was to offer a conception of patriotism, which is not nationalistic; and he primarily focused this concept on loyalty to the state rather than on constitutional rights.[3] He linked it to "militant democracy",[4] democratic order that is capable of defending itself against external and internal enemies through the introduction of potentially illiberal restraints on certain rights.[5]

According to Müller, German constitutional patriotism was initially linked with "militant democracy" (protection/defence of democratic state) and "memory" of the failure of the Weimar Republic. It meant protection and purification against negative historical experiences. Its initial formulations were not very inclusive, they encompassed primarily German citizens. As a form of political attachment, it did not offer solutions to the multicultural predicament. Habermas, however, added a much stronger universalist element to the original conception, focusing more on rights and democratic procedures.[6]

The conception, which Habermas created, also resonated with the past, but primarily with memories of World War II, especially the Holocaust, and attempted to reconsider the political identity of Germany.[7] The overcoming of fascism is the background of forming a post-national identity, centred on universal principles of the rule of law, democracy, and human rights. He aimed at the purification of the public sphere and the promotion of democratic political culture and universalistic moral principles.

He advanced the meaning of constitutional patriotism and spoke about the "post-conventional identities" of individuals, and about the "post-traditional society".

In the post-traditional context, citizens are capable of accepting the universal standpoint of human rights and moral concern, and are asked to reflect critically upon particular traditions and individual experiences/ interests, desires.[8]

---

3 Müller, J.-W., "On the Origins of Constitutional Patriotism", in *Contemporary Political Theory*, 2006, p. 283.

4 *Ibid.*, p. 284.

5 *Ibid.* See also: Preuss, U., "The Constitution of a European Democracy and the Role of the Nation State", in *Ratio Juris*, Vol. 12, Issue 4, December 1999.

6 Müller, J.-W., "On the Origins of Constitutional Patriotism", *op. cit.*, pp. 288-289.

7 Müller, *op. cit.*, p. 291.

8 *Ibid.*, p. 287.

Psychologically de-centred individuals, who relativize what they want in the light of moral concerns, form a post-traditional society which does not suspend religion, tradition or conventional morality, but reconsider them all, "re-interpret (them D.V.) in the light of universalistic claims that have been realized as basic rights and constitutional norms more generally".[9]

There is no unchanging object of identification – either the nation, or, for that matter, a historical constitution. Individuals develop a sense of belonging through deliberation, negotiation, reconsideration, or revision of the given political body. The public sphere is the space of "rationalization of collective identities", of the never-ending process of building and re-building a political identity.[10]

Expectations that this concept would fulfil its capacity just in the case of Germany were however overcome by a differently emerging reality. Constitutional patriotism unexpectedly achieved new prominence in the late 1990s.

Mostly thanks to Habermas' strong influences, it became an attractive model of civic loyalty and membership for democratic legal states and constitutional democracies. The concept became attractive for reconsidering an issue of political identity in view of globalization, migration, multicultural societies, and transitional countries. It started being used as a normative model for understanding the European identity as a supranational political community.

According to Müller, constitutional patriotism designates the idea that political attachment ought to centre on the norms, values, and, more directly, the procedures of a liberal-democratic constitution. It encompasses values such as inclusiveness, individuality and diversity.[11] It refers not only to a written constitution in its entirety (positivist interpretation). It is related to the "constitutional culture" that surrounds every constitution, and includes not merely agreed-upon "constitutional essentials", but also persistent patterns of debate and disagreement about the most faithful interpretation and actual implementation of such essentials.[12]

Fossum diversifies two extreme versions of constitutional patriotism from the point of how much they distance themselves from the nation state and the cultural heredity of the given state's territory and dominant culture: the first is closest to nationalist particularism; the second

9 *Ibid.*

10 *Ibid.*

11 Müller, J.-W., "Three Objections to Constitutional Patriotism", in *Constellations*, Vol. 14, No. 2, 2007, p. 195.

12 *Ibid.*

is closest to cosmopolitanism.[13] He remarks that a whole scale of options related to normative universals exists between these two extremes. He concludes that the second version of constitutional patriotism "...takes us the farthest away and represents a significant departure, dependent as it is on an explicit cosmopolitan constellation, whereas the first version essentially relies on the state form and can operate within a system of states."[14]

An essential feature of constitutional patriotism is its capacity for matching the rising trends of migration and diversification. The point is, firstly, that ethno-cultural conception of an allegiance to the political community by definition does not have the above-mentioned capacity; secondly, ethno-cultural conception cannot circumscribe the changed – multiculturalist – reality, and even more, it easily splits into animosity toward migrants and minorities, who represent "the Other".

Omid Payrow Shabani insists on further advancing the concept of constitutional patriotism for the sake of a multicultural context for the current social and political life. He believes that political theory is lagging behind the radical and rapid changes that are taking place in the world. According to him, today's subject is not a homogeneous citizen of a unilingual, uninational, and unireligious community, but a heterogeneous citizen of a multicultural world. He states that belonging becomes a matter of hybrid identity, rather than the previously conventional permanent one: "Today's communities are... huge multicultural cosmopolitan centers with their Chinatown, little Italy, Indian quarter, and so on. In such transient cities, where hybridism has dissolved the cohesion of any conventional permanence, solidarity cannot be envisaged with respect to a fixed identity as political glue that holds us together."[15]

According to him, the multicultural context of heterogeneous citizens living together fits to the practice of deliberative democracy, democratic constitutionalism and constitutional patriotism.[16]

2. European identity

European identity[17] can be considered in its objective dimension, as being the top-down and bottom-up process of building the transnational

---

13 Fossum, J.E., *op. cit.*, pp. 6-9.

14 *Ibid.*

15 Shabani, O. A. P., "Who is Afraid of Constitutional patriotism?", in *Social Theory and Practice*, Vol. 28, p. 442. See also: Ignatieff, *The Needs of Strangers*, Pinguin Books, New York, 1986.

16 Shabani, O. A. P., "Who is Afraid of Constitutional patriotism?", *op. cit.*, p. 443.

17 See: Vujadinović, D., "On European Identity", in *Synthesis Philosophica*, Zagreb, Croatia 2011.

political community, as well as in its subjective dimension related to the identification of individuals and groups with that political community. The third dimension, related to the relevant interpretative models, has also been an important factor in European identity building. The second and third dimension have two-fold modalities – the ethno-cultural and the civic one.

European polity, as being founded on democratic constitutionalism, has been in a process of completion of its institutional economic, political and legal system. European elites designed and completed the single market, common European currency, the European Central Bank, the Schengen passport free zone, European elections, European symbols – flag, anthem, motto ("united in diversity", or "unity in diversity"), concept and practice of European citizenship. European elites also built a very successful policy of enlargement.

Four basic freedoms are constitutive for European identity; constitutive for that purpose are also universal values and human rights, as well as the practices of networking the Europeans at different micro-levels, like business, finances and the economy, education, cultural entertainment, transnational civic initiatives, European public, I-networking, etc.

EU identity is defined in contrast to the aforementioned traumatic past of Europe (colonialism, imperialism, Nazism, fascism, Stalinism, anti-Semitism), and as a peaceful project oriented towards tolerance, deliberation and compromise. It is also defined in relation to "relevant others", which after the fall of the Berlin Wall and with rising economic changes in a globalized world include besides the U.S.A. also China and India[18] In the internal multicultural context, "relevant others" are economic and political immigrants, members of ethnic and religious minorities, like European inhabitants with a muslim heredity.[19]

In addition, it is defined in relation to multiculturalism, pluralism, and the processes of globalization. Post-colonial and guest workers, as well as other migration waves transformed homogenous national societies into multicultural ones. The uncontrollable character of these immigrations,[20] especially from the 1980s and 1990s forward, caused the formation of the Schengen zone in the 2000s and transformation of Europe into a "fortress" to the outside world.

---

[18] Giddens, E., *Europe in the Global Age*, Belgrade, Clio, 2009.

[19] See: Kermani, N., *Wer ist Wir – Deutschland und seine Muslime*, Verlag C.H. Beck oHG, Munchen, 2010.

[20] Favell, A., "Immigration, Migration, and Free Movement in the Making Europe", in Checkel, J.T. and Katzenstein, P.J. (ed.), *European Identity*, Cambridge University Press 2009, pp. 167-189.

The fall of the Berlin Wall was a push for EU enlargement, which deeply changed the sense and content of the European identity; "new" democracies brought into the European polity and identity-building new forms of diversity, conservatism, ethno-nationalism, as well as the renewed importance of the religion factor.

Revival of Christianity, the importance of which significantly arose by the EU25 enlargement (when Polish Catholicism and Romanian Orthodox religion entered the EU), but also the presence of a significant Muslim minority inside EU countries, puts into question the European secularism.

The signing of the Maastricht Treaty in 1992, with its introducing the notion of European citizenship, represented an important shift in European identity building.

According to Holmes, EU regulations on different micro-levels (for example, in agriculture) and EU networking on different micro-levels (I-networking, European civic initiatives, European art festivals), have become the means by which varied groups of people negotiate over time the common sentiments and expectations that constitute a very broadly based European public space and European identity.[21]

It is better to speak about European identities, about multiple *demoi*; a single European identity is not possible. European identities are open to multiple interpretations; they are not defined primordially from within and cannot be simply imposed politically from without.[22]

There are three main concepts of European-identity building – ethno-cultural (ethno-nationalistic, Euro sceptic), civic (constitutional patriotism) and pluralist (multiculturalist).

The pluralist interpretation could be mainly considered as a version of the civic interpretation, while insisting on matching diversity under an umbrella of universalistic human rights and constitutional principles, and while taking into account the pluralist nature of the European polity. Besides the above mentioned multicultural, pluralist approaches to the European identity issue, which are designated by openness, tolerance, the principle of inclusiveness, and insofar converge with constitutional patriotism (in a sense like Shabani talked about), multicultural solutions of the issue of political identity can also split towards ethno-nationalist collectivist and particularistic solutions.

---

[21] Holmes, D. R., "Experimental Identities (after Maastricht)", in Checkel, J.T. and Katzenstein, P.J. (eds.), *op. cit.*

[22] Katzenstein, P.J. and Checkel, J.T., "Conclusion – European identity in Context", in Checkel, J.T. and Katzenstein, P.J. (eds.), *op. cit.*, p. 226.

In the case of European identity, the ethno-cultural conception has been deeply Euro sceptic. For example, Anthony Smith states that a truly united Europe could have emerged through the slow formation of common European memories, tradition, values, myths and symbols, in the image of ethnos and the nation. He actually does not believe that it is possible at all.[23]

The ethno-cultural interpretation has been essentially linked with the afore-mentioned ethno-nationalistic trends in the "new" Member States. In addition, the ethno-cultural interpretation of European identity helps us to understand the revival of xenophobia and ethno-nationalism in the "old" Member States, which come out as a reaction to mass immigration, globalization, and Europeanization. Patriotic identification with one's own nation state – as opposed to both the common European identity and multiple European identities – is linked to the rising trend of particularism and Euroscepticism.

European constitutional patriotism has to respond to the question of what can attract citizens of Europe to the idea and practice of a united Europe, and how they can achieve it.[24]

3. European Constitutional Patriotism

Constitutional patriotism represents not only the normative model of interpretation and allegiance to the EU, but also the constitutional-institutional reality of the EU. In the Constitutional Treaty, Article 1-2, it was written: "The Union is founded on the values of respect for human dignity, liberty, democracy, equality, the rule of law and respect for human rights…"[25]

Habermas and Müller mostly develop the concept of European constitutional patriotism. However, in a rising trend of its considering, other authors – like Calhun, Walker, Baubock, Kostakopoulou – tend to widen this concept in order to make it more inclusive and open for differences, for overcoming the "solidarity gap".

In an attempt to define European constitutional patriotism, Habermas and Müller pose the question – how can constitutional culture, as developed to a certain extent in the European nation states, be transformed into a

23 Jovanovic, M., "In Search of a European Identity", in Jovanovic, M., Vujadinović, D. and Etinski, R. (eds.), *Human Rights and Democracy in the EU*, Belgrade/Maribor, 2009.

24 Habermas, J., *The Divided West*, Polity Press 2006, p. 76.

25 Kumm, M., "The idea of Thick Constitutional Patriotism and Its Implications for the Role and Structure of European legal History", in *German Law Journal*, Vol. 06, No. 02, p. 320.

sense of belonging and attachment to the European polity? Constitutional patriotism as linked to nation states is presupposed, but it also has to be overcome, accommodated and transformed in accordance with the supranational context.

Habermas states that the real issue is conditions that must be fulfilled if the citizens are to be able to extend their civic solidarity beyond their respective national borders, with a goal of achieving mutual inclusion. The civic conception of "the nation" – as opposed to an ethnic one – "reflects both the actual historical trajectory of the European nation-states and the fact that democratic citizenship is established as abstract, legally mediated solidarity between strangers".[26]

Habermas believes that the change of focus from identification with the state to an orientation towards the constitution leads to a relative uncoupling of the constitution from the state.[27] As regards the question of a possible extension of civic solidarity beyond national boundaries, Habermas remarks that the functioning of the United Nations in preventing human rights violations and peacekeeping shows the beginnings of communicative structures of the global public sphere. However, this narrow basis of legitimacy and common potential for solid reactions and actions is not sufficient to integrate the European Union.[28]

He tries to identify shared, common elements of European mentality, political culture, political morality, which are "supportive dispositions" for a "pan-European discourse". These are related to the features of a peaceful and cooperative Europe, open to other cultures, ready to engage in dialogue, capable of dealing in a compromising way with its incomparable cultural diversity, capable of pacifying class conflicts through the welfare state, and ready for self-restriction of state sovereignty in the context of the EU.

Europe had to learn "painful lessons how differences can be communicated, oppositions institutionalized, and tensions stabilized". According to him, traits of shared political morality came to life in the third quarter of the 20th century (the "Golden Age"), related to "the recognition of differences, the mutual recognition of others in their otherness". As empirical manifestations of shared identity or European mentality he also mentions the advance of secularization, high level of confidence in the organizational accomplishments and steering capacities of the state, scepticism towards effectiveness of the market, a sharp sense for the "dialectic

26 Jovanovic, M., *op. cit.*, p. 57.

27 Habermas, J., *The Divided West*, *op. cit.*, p. 79.

28 *Ibid.*, p. 80.

of enlightenment", and a desire for a multilateral and legally regulated international order.[29]

Habermas identified five attributes which Europeans share: the neutrality of authority, embodied in the separation of church and state; trust in politics rather than the capitalist market; an ethos of solidarity in the fight for social justice; high esteem for international law and the rights of the individual and support for the organizational and leading role of the state.[30] He tries to investigate how sustainable these shared features are, and believes that in order for post-war European mentality to emerge more clearly, the further development of a pan-European discourse is necessary – a European public space.

In his most recently published book in 2012, *The Crisis of the European Union: A Response*,[31] he speaks of "the expectation that the growing mutual trust among European peoples will give rise to a transnational, though attenuated, form of civic solidarity among citizens of the Union".[32]

The key for Habermas is the formation of a transnational public space. He says that this process of consciousness formation cannot be controlled from above, or produced by administrative decision.[33] An identity-shaping internal dynamic of public discourse at a European level is possible, and was present in deliberations over conflicts of interests about the Iraq war, health-care reform, and immigration policy.[34] The global crisis and the Euro zone crisis open new spaces for a public discourse on European issues.

Habermas speaks of the lack of awareness among Europeans about how immensely and deeply they have had a common destiny/fate, how big advantages of the monetary union, visa liberation and many other things have been on the agenda. He remarks that the irresponsible behaviour of European intellectuals contributed to this lack of awareness and to an insufficiently developed mutual trust among Europeans.

> I think it is sufficient to cite a couple of concrete demographic and economic statistics to remind ourselves of the diminishing weights of Europe in the

29 *Ibid.*, pp. 43-45.

30 *Ibid.*

31 The magazine *The Global Journal* published his interview with Francis Fukuyama on May 18, 2012, under the title: "The European Citizen: Just a Myth?" (http://theglobaljournal.net/article/view/695/).

32 Habermas, J., *The Crisis of the European Union, A Response*, English ed., Polity Press, 2012.

33 Interview, "The European Citizen: Just a Myth?", *op. cit.*

34 *Ibid.*

> world and to ask ourselves whether we must not pull ourselves together if we want to remain in a position to defend our cultural and social forms of life against the leveling force of the global economy – and, most importantly, to maintain a certain amount of influence on the international political agenda in accordance with our universalistic conceptions.[35]

Weiler's model of supra-national citizenship as a combination of national and European citizenship states that these two citizenships have to stay distinct and complementary. He argues for a multiple identity and multiple *demoi*, where individuals simultaneously express both organic-cultural identification with their nation and membership to European supranational values that transcend ethno-cultural differences.[36]

Like Habermas, Jan-Werner Müller states that European constitutional patriotism and nation states' constitutional patriotisms inform and mutually enrich each other. He states that "European nation" and "European constitutional patriotism" depends on the "European public sphere", and would also partly have to create that public sphere.[37] However, he thinks that the Holocaust memory cannot be formative in the case of European identity, if it should be inclusive enough for immigrants and minorities. Militant democracy could however play the role when liberal democracy in some of the EU states does face real danger.

He thinks that European constitutional patriotism should be centred on constitutional identity, e.g. on universalistic liberal democratic values and practices, refracted and interpreted through particular historical experiences. He believes that the EU has developed these principles and practices as part of a distinctive constitutional identity.[38]

He speaks about multi-levelled processes of European identification, dependent on particular problems or projects, rather than building "collective European identity"; this however does not exclude, according to him, the possibility of the emergence of this new type of collective identity as well.[39]

---

35 *Ibid.*

36 See: Müller, J.-W., *European Constitutional Patriotism*, Princeton University Press, 2007 (quotations according to the Serbian translation of the book, published by Fabrika knjiga, Belgrade, 2010).

37 Müller, J.-W., "A 'Thick' Constitutional Patriotism for the EU? On Morality, Memory and Militancy", http://www.princeton.edu/~jmueller/CP-ThickCPEurope-JWMueller.pdf.

38 *Ibid.*, p. 20.

39 See also: Katzenstein, P.J. and Checkel, J.T., Conclusion – European identity in Context, in Checkel, J.T. and Katzenstein, P.J. (eds.), *op. cit.*, p. 213.

Müller lists three peculiar characteristics, which distinguish the EU as a specific and innovative kind of transnational polity: firstly, its constitutionalization has been an open-ended process of deliberation and political struggle; secondly, continuity exists between the liberal-democratic character of the European nation-states and the EU itself; thirdly, continuity exists between constitutional patriotisms of the European nation-states and European constitutional patriotism.

He says that the EU constitution is an ongoing project, and EU polity is not based on pre-existing civic solidarities, but on mutually agreed upon projects and enterprises. Further, this process is open not just with regard to its ultimate outcome; it is also open with regard to its constituents. The European constituent power itself is subject to enlargement. The EU is not based on one constituent power, or one *demos*. Instead, it is based on an expanding group of *demoi*.[40] It is not about creating a basic identity, which supports a constitution, but about a dynamic and complex process of "sharing identities", while at the same time tolerating and preserving differences.[41]

According to Müller, the constitutional architecture of the EU's ability to maintain the diversity of nation states represents peaceful continuity with their liberal-democratic character and the simultaneous overcoming of their particularisms. The constitution making of the European polity is based on deliberation and political struggles without a unique purpose proposed in advance; normative constitutional culture has been in this case a continuous project in contrast to the well-defined nation state constitutional orders.

The normative and economic attractiveness of the European polity arises from the fact that its constituting power is capable of enlargement and is capable of the "transnational overflowing" toward countries which are outside of the EU. The attractiveness of the EU also comes from its openness and weak bonds. European people are attracted by the Union and tend towards it in a measure of its stimulating diversity and not by imposing homogeneity and unity. European peoples will continuously have to negotiate, and will have to decide how much they wish to share in common, and how much they wish to keep apart.[42]

Müller accepts Weiler's requirement for "constitutional tolerance", and discusses the "silent cosmopolitan revolution" that has transformed nation-states, as opposed to superseding them with a "supra-nation state".

---

40 Müller, J.-W., *European Constitutional Patriotism*, *op. cit.*, p. 140.

41 Müller, J.-W., "A 'Thick' Constitutional Patriotism for the EU? On Morality, Memory and Militancy", *op. cit.*, p. 21.

42 Müller, J.-W., *European Constitutional Patriotism*, *op. cit.*, pp. 138-146.

He remarks that the Union demands all peoples to learn from each other against a background of the persistent multitude, as well as that the attractiveness of the European polity also comes from multi-level governance, a lack of one power centre above the nation-states.[43]

Europeans do not feel the call for obedience; they are attracted by advantages of the European polity but are not passionately identified with it. The ideal of mutual recognition of different *demoi* and celebrating diversity is very attractive, but it bears the risk of converting European trans-national multiculturalism into plural monoculturalism. The attractiveness of the European polity produces loyalty and conviction, which has always been open for criticism and contestation.

European constitutional patriotism is an existent example of reflexive, self-critical belonging without weakening the community, but also without any strong identification with that community. It promises a combination of critical reflection and complex emotional attachment to the political community.[44]

In contrast to the notion of constitutional patriotism related to the nation-state, which bears full respect for the clearly defined constitutional principles and well established constitutions of the given nation-states, it reflects the motto "Unity in diversity", a meaning of self-critical belonging, loyalty without passionate identification, e.g. as much loyalty as benefits have been given and are available. It also reflects the genuine character of the EU as the never-ending building process of a genuine democratic trans-national polity, as based on universalistic principles and democratic procedures.

Müller, like Habermas, says that the decisive question is how these principles could be made clearer in the eyes of the public, more obvious, more visible. He emphasizes the responsibility of intellectuals and elites to clarify the benefits of the European polity to the public.

Craig Calhoun points to the fact that constitutional patriotism fits with multiple conceptions of the good life in modern societies, that it is compatible with different constitutional arrangements, and that it bears a careful balance between a commitment to universal principles and the recognition of particularity. Like Habermas and Müller, he points to the crucial importance of the public sphere for promoting constitutional patriotism and European identity.[45]

---

43 *Ibid.*, p. 149.

44 *Ibid.*, pp. 167-8.

45 Calhoun, C., "Constitutional Patriotism and the Public Sphere: Interests, Identity, and Solidarity in the Integration of Europe", published online, 14 November 2006, p. 278.

According to him, constitutional patriotism has difficulty in overcoming the "solidarity gap". A shared political culture based on human rights and an active public sphere is decisive for turning strangers into fellow citizens, and for overcoming problems of solidarity and imbalance between universalistic intentions and recognition of particularities.

Neil Walker adds to this discourse the notion of constitutional pluralism. Constitutionalism must not remain too state-centred; it must become more open for social developments associated with the politics of difference. The point is that the post-Westphalian configuration is plural, unlike the one-dimensional Westphalian one, while the units are no longer isolated, constitutionally self-sufficient monads like nation states.[46]

The constitutional dimension of EU law poses the most pressing paradigm challenging test to the so-called constitutional monism related to the Westphalian age, and for accepting constitutional pluralism. The mentioned pluralism, by contrast, recognizes that the European order has developed beyond the traditional confines of inter-*national* law and now has independent constitutional claims, which exist alongside the continuing claims of states.[47]

Walker also points to the change that has taken place in regards to sovereignty. He says that the claim of sovereignty of the EU over a range of competences previously within exclusive jurisdiction of the EU member states does not seriously question the continuing sovereignty of the member states in respect of their territorial jurisdiction. He adds, however, that the member states' sovereignty may become "significantly, imprecisely and progressively limited".[48]

He remarks that the change occurs alongside a change to the meaning of citizenship. Within modern constitutional discourse, citizenship cannot anymore be exclusively bound to and by the state. After the Maastricht Treaty, it has its important expressions in the legal status of European citizenship.[49]

According to Baubock, identities in modern democratic polities, including the EU, are shaped by multiple overlapping and changing affiliations of different social groups and associations, among which the most important are the ones related to gender, sexual, political, and ideological

---

46 Walker, N., "The Idea of Constitutional Pluralism", in *The Modern Law Review*, Vol. 65, No. 3, May 2002, p. 355.

47 *Ibid.*, p. 337.

48 *Ibid.*, p. 346. See also: MacCormick, "Beyond the Sovereign State", in *The Modern Law Review*, Vol. 56, No. 1, January 1993, p. 1.

49 Walker, N., "The Idea of Constitutional Pluralism", *op. cit.*, p. 351.

orientation, religious conviction, as well as class, language, and ethnicity. "In such polities, democratic representation and citizenship has to combine the traditional liberal precept of equal rights for equal citizens with sensitivity for those collective identities."[50] It implies measures for "symbolic recognition" of a minority or immigrant community's culture and the allocation of resources for enabling these communities to develop without being subjected to either coercive assimilation or enforced segregation.

He thinks that European identity cannot be based only on constitutional rights of Union citizens, but must extend pluralism in the EU beyond the mere recognition of national identities to acknowledging the collective identities of sub-national and transnational minorities. Institutional measures would be related to direct EU measures that go beyond existent nation-state non-discrimination and directly allocate group-differentiated rights, material resources and political powers to specifically disadvantaged groups.

The Greek author Kostakopoulou also offered an idea of a more inclusive European polity, multiple identities, and the concept of a constructive, responsible EU citizenship. According to her, European citizenship should be a common concern for the future of a pluralist political community. Formal inclusion of third-country nationals who live and work in the EU should be regulated by a Community law concept, and without requiring them to possess the nationality of an individual Member State.[51] In addition, political democracy has to become more participatory and inclusive, and social policy has to be more just in respect to disadvantaged social groups. She calls on responsible citizens to fight against the restrictive immigration and asylum measures, which are coming to life in many Member States. She calls for an "ethos of responsibility and respect", and for "virtuous citizenship based on an ethic of the Other."[52]

Conclusion

Evidently, European constitutional patriotism has had its germs in the constitutional culture of the Europeans. Equally evidently, still it has been more declarative, ideal-typical model than reality in a full sense. The crucial problem is a European public sphere that is far from fully developed. The rising economic crisis and crisis of European integrity, identity crisis, and crisis of the Euro zone endangers further development of European constitutional patriotism.

---

50 Baubock, R., "Citizenship and national Identities in the European Union", in *Harvard Jean Monnet Working Papers* 4/1997.

51 See: Jovanovic, M., In Search of a European identity, *op. cit.*, p. 63.

52 *Ibid.*, p. 65.

It is the responsibility of European intellectuals to clarify the context of the crisis, to explain the reality of a common destiny for Europeans, and to accentuate the necessity of solving the crisis from the point of European public reason and European constitutional patriotism. Focusing on divisions and particular interests among the nation-states and their publics cannot bring a sustainable solution.

There are, according to Habermas,[53] strong reasons for staying together and for defending cultural and social forms of common life and shared values and principles in accordance with emerging constitutional culture. Namely, maintaining an influence of the EU on international politics exactly depends on that.

Claus Offe affirms a similar and complementary form of argumentation. According to him, economic and political measures necessary for solving the current economic, political, and identity crisis shall require the civic solidarity of all Europeans, agreement upon the measures which would fit the interests of all, and not only of the citizens of either debtor countries or of the indebted countries. This presupposes and imposes debt mutualisation in the long run and on a large scale, with massive redistributive measures between member-states and classes. It means that austerity measures would have not rest mostly on the debtor nations' shoulders, and on the lower classes, but the creditor countries and richer classes would have been strongly and justly affected by appropriate redistributive and austerity measures as well.[54]

The survival of the European polity depends on capacities for solving the crisis from the point of European solidarity, backed by universalistic principles and democratic procedures, as well as by the democratic political culture and European public space. It is necessary to promote inclusiveness, tolerance, and multiple identities based on both universal human rights and constitutional principles and their balancing with and accommodating for differences and particularities. In other words, public reasoning from the point of European constitutional patriotism is essentially needed and important. Ideal-typically speaking, the survival of the European polity really depends on the capacities of EU agents to solve the current crisis from the point of principles and procedures of European constitutional patriotism.

---

53 Habermas, J., *The Crisis of the European Union, A Response*, *op. cit.*

54 Offe, C., "Europe Entrapped: Does the European Union Have the Political Capacity to Overcome its Current Crisis?", in Jovanovic, M. and Vujadinović, D. (eds.), *Identity, Political and Human Rights Culture as Prerequisites of Constitutional Democracy*, Eleven International Publishing, Amsterdam, 2013.

However, the question stays open whether European elites can overcome nation-state particularisms, party ideologies and particularistic interests in order to achieve public reasoning in the common EU interest; whether public deliberation on the European level and European public space can or cannot come strongly to life, in order to overcome the deep crisis and the threat of an overall collapse. The question will stay dangerously open and with destructive capacities. However, social movements and European peoples, *demoi*, could and should start offering more clear and powerful demands and responses related to overcoming the deep economic, political and social crisis. They might impose such a kind of pressure over elites and power-centres of the EU, which eventually could result in favour of much more social Europe, the one less declaratively and more substantially based on European constitutional patriotism.

Europeanization of Constitutional Standards of Freedom of Association Restrictions*

Tanasije MARINKOVIĆ

1. Introduction

Contemporary development of human rights law is marked by two mutually stimulating and ever growing trends. One is the interplay between the international and national legal systems leading to the internationalization of constitutionally entrenched fundamental rights and constitutionalization of international human rights law. The other trend is the judicialization of human rights law both on the international and national scale, as manifested by the existence of the international human rights courts and by the expansion of constitutional courts' jurisdiction in the field of fundamental rights protection. The end result of these processes has been the general emboldening of the courts as decision-makers, on both levels, and the emergence of a judge-made human rights law. These trends have been particularly prominent under the jurisdiction of the European Court of Human Rights (ECtHR), where, through a vertical and horizontal cooperation between the Strasbourg court on the one side, and the national supreme/constitutional courts, on the other, European human rights law is being developed.

This paper discusses the creation of the ECtHR case-law on the freedom of association restrictions demonstrating not only how the European human rights law is judge-made and legitimized, but also how far-reaching these changes are substantially, i.e. how much they challenge the long standing constitutional concepts. The case of the praetorian refinement of the conditions for the dissolution of political organizations is all the more pertinent, in terms of the aforementioned structural processes, when taking into account that the ECtHR has considered that only convincing and compelling reasons can justify restrictions on parties' freedom of association,

* This article is a result of the work on the Project "Constitutionalism and Rule of Law in the Nation-State Building – the Case of Serbia", funded by the Ministry of Science of the Republic of Serbia.

and that in determining whether those reasons are present, "the Contracting States have only a limited margin of appreciation, which goes hand in hand with rigorous European supervision embracing both the law and the decisions applying it, including those given by independent courts".[1]

In contrast to these principles, throughout the Twentieth century – "the short Twentieth century" in Hobsbawm's words – the European constitutional practice in the field of freedom of association restrictions was openly illiberal. The banning and dissolution of political parties and other political organizations was considered as one of the legitimate instruments in the arsenal of the "militant democracy". Parallel to the recognition and protection of the right to association, post-World War I and particularly post-World War II European legislation provided conditions for its limitation, including the closure of associations. This approach was a reaction to the abuse of political rights and democratic mechanisms in the inter-war period when democracy and democratic tolerance were used for their own destruction, as "the Trojan horse by which the enemy enters the city".[2] Loewenstein was one of the first to recognize the "democratic dilemma" (namely, how could democracy address itself to curtailing fair play for all opinions and free speech without destroying the very basis of its existence and justification?), and to advocate against this "legalistic self-complacency and suicidal lethargy", by proposing appropriate measures for combating subversive extremism. The most comprehensive and effective of these measures, by which democracy becomes militant, consists, according to Loewenstein, in proscribing subversive movements, parties, groups and associations.[3]

Following this reasoning, many political parties and organizations were banned in Europe, either through a statutory proscription, or administrative/judicial dissolution, as a way of repression of ideological and political enemies. Even when the statutory proscription was not open, as it was the case with the *ex lege* banning of fascist and/or communist parties, the conditions for the administrative/judicial dissolution were often imprecisely couched and lacked the due process of law safeguards. The French 1936 Statute on fighting groups and private militias (*Loi sur les groupes de combat et les milices privées*) and its application are a typical case of militant democracy in action. Under this legislation, in the Fifth

1 *United Communist Party of Turkey and Others v. Turkey*, Nos. 133/1996/752/951, para. 46, 30 January 1998.

2 Loewenstein, K., "Militant Democracy and Fundamental Rights I", 31 *The American Political Science Review*, 3/1937, 424.

3 Loewenstein, K., "Militant Democracy and Fundamental Rights II", 31 *The American Political Science Review*, 4/1937, 646.

Republic alone, the President banned no fewer than 45 political parties, movements and other organizations.[4] Other notable examples of the freedom of association restrictions in the spirit of militant democracy were the dissolutions of the German national-socialist party (*Sozialistische Reichspartei*) in 1952, and Communist party (*Kommunistische Partei Deutschlands*) in 1956, by the Federal Constitutional Court.[5]

Acting in synergy with the national supreme/constitutional courts, the ECtHR introduced an entirely new approach in the field of political organizations' dissolution, notably through its "Turkish case-law". This approach is characterized by a careful examination of the "necessity in democratic society" principle, i.e. whether there is "pressing social need" for the dissolution, and whether such a measure is "proportional".[6] Offering its response to the Loewenstein's "democratic dilemma", the ECtHR thereby brought the European constitutional jurisprudence on freedom of association restrictions closer to the United States Supreme Court balancing test of "clear and present danger", known for its liberty-oriented approach, even in relation to extremist speech.[7]

The first section of the paper looks into how the European human rights law emerged through a dialogue between European and national judges, placing this process in a more general context of internationalization of constitutional law and constitutionalization of international law. The second section illustrates these structural features of the European human rights law with a development of the ECtHR case law on the freedom association restriction.

4 Mbongo, P., "Actualité et renouveau de la loi du 10 janvier 1936 sur les groupes de combat et les milices privées", 3 *Revue du droit public* 1998, pp. 721-722. *See also*, Esplugas, P., "L'interdiction des partis politiques", 36 *Revue française de Droit constitutionnel* 1998, pp. 673-709.

5 *See*, Thiel, M., "Germany", in Thiel, M. (ed.), *The 'Militant Democracy'– Principle in Modern Democracies*, ed. Ashgate, Farnham 2009, pp. 107-145.

6 The 1950 European Convention on Human Rights, which established the ECtHR, provides that "everyone has the right to freedom of peaceful assembly and to freedom of associations with others", adding to it that "no restrictions shall be placed on the exercise of these rights other than such as are prescribed by law and are *necessary in a democratic society* in the interests of the national security or public safety, for the prevention of disorder or crime, for the protection of health or morals or for the protection of rights and freedoms of others" (Art. 11 (1) and (2), emphasis added).

7 The Court has held since Brandenburg v. Ohio, 395 U.S. 444, 447 (1968) that advocacy becomes unlawful incitement only "where such advocacy is directed to inciting or producing imminent lawlessness and is likely to incite or produce such action". And it reinforced this position by striking down a "hate speech" ordinance as impermissible content regulation, R.A.V. v. St. Paul, 112 S.Ct. 2538 (1992).

2. Structural Features of the European Human Rights Law

2.1. Internationalization of Constitutional Law and Constitutionalization of International Law

Globalization and democratization trends have had profound effects on an increasing interplay between international and constitutional law. The intensified economic and cultural cross-border activities, as a result of liberalization of world markets and of the third wave of democratization, but also, and above all, the efforts to establish global peace and security after the atrocities of World War II, required a new public international law and constitutional law framework. These mutually stimulating developments took the form, *inter alia*, of the internationalization of constitutional law and of the constitutionalization of public international law. At the very heart of this was the emergence of a new branch of law – human rights law – both nationally and internationally. The signing of the UN Charter, followed by other UN and regional human rights documents, marked, in that respect, the beginning of a new era. They reflected, although not always consciously, a profound shift in the assumptions of sovereignty, by piercing the territorial veil of the state.[8] Individuals were no longer to be taken care of, on the international level, *qua* members of a group, a minority, or another category. They began to be protected *qua* single human beings. Thereby, the arrival of human rights on the international scene proved, indeed, to be a subversive event, forcing states to give account of the activities which were only a few decades earlier their exclusive authority (e.g. how they treat their nationals, administer justice, run prisons, and so on).[9]

The internationalization of constitutional law has taken place through the vertical and horizontal convergence of international law norms and constitutional texts, as well as of the case law of the (quasi-)judicial bodies entrusted with their enforcement.[10] The vertical convergence results from the incorporation of international human rights treaties into domestic constitutions (e.g. Canadian Charter of Rights and Freedoms incorporates two international covenants – on Civil and Political Rights and on Economic, Social and Cultural Rights, while no fewer than 15 international human

---

8 Bobbitt, Ph., "Public International Law", in D. Patterson (ed.), *A Companion to Philosophy of Law and Legal Theory*, Blackwell Publishing, Malden, Oxford, Carlton, 2005, pp. 106-107.

9 Cassese, A., *International Law*, Oxford University Press, Oxford 2005, p. 375.

10 Peters, A., & Preuss, U. K., "International Relations and International Law", in M. Tushnet, Th. Fleiner, & Ch. Saunders (eds.), *Routledge Handbook of Constitutional Law*, Routledge, London and New York 2013, pp. 34-35.

rights documents are annexed to the Constitution of Bosnia and Herzegovina), or from the drafting of the constitutions, typically of new democracies, in a way that mirrors the provisions of international treaties (e.g. South African or Central and Eastern European constitutions).[11] Furthermore, these and other constitutions usually provide for the direct applicability of international human rights treaties, ranking them commonly above legislative norms, and sometimes even on an equal footing with constitutional provisions. The processes of vertical convergence came to completion with an effective domestic enforcement of the given rules and principles, where the case-law of the international human rights courts (ECtHR and Inter-American Court of Human Rights) is treated as a binding source, profiling international human rights law and constitutionally entrenched fundamental rights as a single body of norms.

These trends have naturally been accompanied by various types of horizontal convergences, i.e. comparativism across constitutional jurisdictions. As the constitutional charters of human rights became reflective of the international human rights documents, and thereby of one another (convergence of constitutions *inter se*), the constitutional justices of different states received an unprecedented opportunity to learn from each other, even in interpreting their own constitutional clauses.[12] And although the most active participants in this cross-jurisdictional dialogue have been the constitutional justices *inter se*, a similar type of exchanges has developed between international human rights courts themselves, as well as between international and constitutional jurisdictions, where the case-law of one jurisdiction is considered as a resource (and not as a source) of another.

Constitutionalization of public international law, both as an empirical fact, and a normative claim, became a prominent feature of the international legal order with the shift of public decision-making away from nation-states, towards international organizations. This process has been manifested in the evolution of international law from a law of coordination between loosely affiliated states, to a law of close cooperation which goes far into the realm of traditionally domestic concerns and produces direct effects on the individuals of the given member-states.[13] Hence, the "constitutionalization of public international law" does not only describe a progressive development of international legal order, but also expresses

---

11 Chang, W.-C., & Yeh, J.-R., "Internationalization of Constitutional Law", in M. Rosenfeld & A. Sajo (eds.), *The Oxford Handbook of Comparative Constitutional Law*, Oxford University Press, Oxford 2012, pp. 1167-1168.

12 *Id.*, p. 1169.

13 De Wet, E., "The Constitutionalization of Public International Law", in M. Rosenfeld & A. Sajo (eds.), *The Oxford Handbook of Comparative Constitutional Law*, Oxford University Press, Oxford 2012, pp. 1210-1211.

the need for legal restrictions on and the democratic control of the exercise of public powers on the international level.[14]

The aforementioned changes and concerns have particularly been accentuated in the context of the evolution of the European Community (EC)/European Union (EU) law. Namely, neither the Paris Treaty, nor the Rome Treaty, by which the European Communities were established, contained any allusion to the protection of human rights. And yet, once the European Court of Justice (ECJ) put in place its constitutional jurisprudence in *Van Gend en Loos* and *Costa v. Enel*, it became an imperative to find a way to vindicate human rights at the EC level. For, "how could one assert the direct effect and supremacy of European law – vesting huge constitutional power in the organs of the Community – without postulating embedded legal and judicial guaranties on the exercise of such power?".[15] As a result, the ECJ took the initiative to recognize fundamental rights as part of the EC system: the "general principles" were employed as the legal means for the introduction of human rights in the EU legal order; the declared sources of interpretation to give content to these general principles were the "constitutional tradition common to the member states" and the European Convention on Human Rights; and, not only did the ECJ enforce human rights against EC/EU institutions, but it also supervised their application by the national authorities as well.[16]

2.2. European Human Rights Law as a Supranational Judge-Made Law[17]

However, the most comprehensive developments, in terms of internationalisation of constitutionally entrenched fundamental rights and constitutionalization of international human rights law, have occurred under the jurisdiction of the ECtHR, established by the European Convention on Human Rights. While it is undisputed that the formal traits of this law place it within the domain of international law, its essential features, some of which are the praetorian work of the ECtHR, correspond

14 *Id.*, p. 1211; Peters & Preuss, pp. 35-36.

15 Weiler, J. H. H., *The Constitution of Europe – "Do the new clothes have an emperor?" and other essays on European integration*, Cambridge University Press, Cambridge 1999, pp. 107-108.

16 Torres Pérez, A., *Conflicts of Rights in the European Union – A Theory of Supranational Adjudication*, Oxford University Press, Oxford 2009, p. 35.

17 Subsection 2.2. is partially reproduced from: Ribičič, C., Nenadić, B., & Marinković, T., "Multilevel System of Human Rights Protection in Europe – A View from Central and Eastern Europe", in L. R. Basta Fleiner & T. Marinković (eds.), *Key Developments in Constitutionalism and Constitutional Law*, Eleven International Publishing, Den Haag, 2014 (forthcoming).

to the concept of the contemporary judicial review of constitutionality. Concerning the former, it should be pointed out: first and foremost, that High Contracting Parties to the Convention are States which have accepted the limited jurisdiction of the ECtHR in their mutual disputes, and those which an individual may bring before the ECtHR against one or more of the Contracting States; and, second, that the structural relationship between the ECtHR and national courts cannot be equated to the hierarchical relationship between the higher courts and lower courts in the Member States. As to the latter, a number of elements indicate it: substantially, functionally and structurally the Convention can be assimilated to a constitutional bill of rights; the introduction of the judicial protection of the Convention, comparable to the judicial review of constitutionality; direct access of individuals to the ECtHR through application, akin to the access to the constitutional courts through constitutional complaint; advancement by the ECtHR of different techniques of interpretation, which resemble the constitutional courts' judicial activism.[18] Hence, the complexities of European human rights law and its dual nature, namely, the international law side of its basis and structure, and the constitutional law side of its content and process, which make it a supranational law.[19]

It is obvious that these developments in European human rights law, notably judge-made law, cannot be explained in one-dimensional terms, by reference to national delegation, intergovernmentalism and the traditional law of international organizations. To try to explain the new emerging post-Westphalian order in these terms is "to force square pegs into round holes, and to understate the extent and distort the character of the transformation which is underway".[20] Instead, for epistemic purposes, a pluralistic approach has to be undertaken which abandons state-centeredness and accepts that in the post-Westphalian world there exists a range of different constitutional sites (European and Member States) and processes (in particular, the judicial processes) configured in a heterarchical rather than hierarchical pattern.[21] In contrast to constitutional monism, which knows only of states as the sole centres

18 On the ECtHR's different techniques of interpretation, *see*: Popović, D., *The Emergence of the European Human Rights Law*, Eleven International Publishing, Den Haag, 2011.

19 For more information, *see*: Marinković, T., "Pravna priroda evropskog prava ljudskih prava" ([Legal Nature of the European Human Rights Law], in R. Vasić & I. Krstić (eds.), *Razvoj pravnog sistema Srbije i harmonizacija sa pravom EU, prilozi projektu 2012* [*Development of the Legal System of Serbia and harmonization with the EU Law: Contributions to the 2012 Project*], Faculty of Law University of Belgrade, Belgrade, 2013, pp. 88-96.

20 Walker, N., "The Idea of Constitutional Pluralism", *The Modern Law Review*, Vol. 65, No. 3, 2002, p. 337.

21 *Id.*, p. 317.

or units of constitutional authority, constitutional pluralism "recognizes that the European order [...] has developed beyond the traditional confines of inter-national law and now makes its own independent constitutional claims, and that these claims exist alongside the continuing claims of states".[22]

In the context of European human rights law, constitutional pluralism indicates the absence of hierarchy between the foundational constitutional documents of the interacting national and supranational legal orders. And, although a pluralist framework might look too precarious to be sustainable, the national and supranational orders are so closely intertwined that the interdependence of goals and functions will secure the continuity of the community.[23] The key players, supranational and national, in this process are the courts, the ECtHR and ECJ, on the one hand, and the constitutional/supreme courts, on the other, who have a common mission: to protect and develop human rights within their own respective arenas.[24]

"Both EU and ECHR human rights law are, in one way or another, binding on the domestic legal system and must be co-applied by the national court in the process of constitutional adjudication. In effect, the high European courts and the high domestic jurisdictions are dealing with similar matters, applying the similar provisions of substantive law, and following the similar procedural rules".[25] Hence the importance of dialogue and co-operation between the two jurisdictional levels that, in the context of the pluralist legal structure of the EU and ECHR, secures the legitimacy of European human rights law and its effectiveness.[26]

3. Development of the Convention Case-Law on the Freedom of Association Restrictions

3.1. Turkish Constitutional Court's Case-Law on the Dissolution of Political Parties

Although militant democracy is particularly associated with the Federal Republic of Germany, which elaborated its most comprehensive mechanisms in its 1949 Basic Law, and put them in place, notably by the

[22] *Id.*, p. 337.

[23] Torres Pérez, p. 69.

[24] *See*: Garlicki, L., "Cooperation of courts: The role of supranational jurisdictions in Europe", *ICON*, Vol. 6, No. 3 & 4, 2008, p. 522.

[25] *Id.*, p. 511.

[26] Torres Pérez, p. 97, argues that judicial dialogue is the source of legitimacy of supranational adjudication in the EU, and Garlicki, p. 521, claims that "the Strasbourg court cannot function without a constant dialogue with and the support of the domestic courts".

Federal Constitutional Court rulings on the dissolution of the neo-Nazi and communist parties in the 1950s, the practice of judicial closure of political parties, in the spirit of militant democracy, was most developed in Turkey. As a matter of fact, it is the practice of the Turkish Constitutional Court, more than any other, which served the ECtHR to formulate its standards of the freedom of association restrictions.[27]

Most of the Constitutional Court's dissolutions, which eventually ended up before the ECtHR, date back to the period between 1991 and 1997. All eight Constitutional Court rulings from that period concerned the Kurdish parties which were dissolved on the same, eminently illiberal, grounds. In reaching its decision in the ruling, the Constitutional Court noted that these parties referred in their political message to two nations – the Kurdish nation and the Turkish nation, claiming for the Kurdish national and cultural rights, with the purpose of creating minorities, and ultimately establishing a Kurdish-Turkish federation, to the detriment of the unity of the Turkish nation.[28] Furthermore, in almost all of these cases the Court established that in the calls to self-determination of the Kurds and to "war for independence" there were similarities with the acts of terrorist organizations, despite the difference in means, and all this, according to the Court, had led to tolerance and excuse of terrorist acts and had had characteristics of incitement to insurrection.[29] In one case (*United Communist Party of Turkey*), the name of the party itself was controversial,[30] while in another one (*The Freedom and Democracy Party*) the dissolution was justified by the violation of the principle of secularism, due to the proposal for the abolition of the Religious Affairs

---

27 Hence, "la jurisprudence [...] *essentiellement turque*" of the ECtHR. Dhommeaux, J., "La société démocratique européenne: légitimité et participation dans la jurisprudence de la Cour européenne des droits de l'homme", in *Légitimité du pouvoir politique et représentation*, Edition Cujas, Paris 2008, p. 155 (emphasis added).

28 Rulings of the Turkish Constitutional Court are cited according to their reference in the pertinent judgments of the ECtHR. *United Communist Party of Turkey and Others v. Turkey*, para. 10; *Parti socialiste et autres c. Turquie*, Nos. 20/1997/804/1007, para. 15, 25 mai 1998; *Freedom and Democracy Party (OZDEP) v. Turkey*, No. 23885/94, para. 14, 8 December 1999; *Yazar and Others v. Turkey*, Nos. 22723/93, 22724/93 and 22725/93, para. 22, 9 April 2002; *Dicle pour le Parti de la démocratie (DEP) c. Turquie*, No. 25141/94, para. 22, 10 December 2002; *Parti socialiste de Turquie (STP) et autres c. Turquie*, No. 26482/95, para. 18, 12 novembre 2003; *Parti de la démocratie et de l'évolution et autres c. Turquie*, Nos. *39210/98 et 39974/98*, paras. 12-14, 26 avril 2006; *Emek Partisi et Senol c. Turquie*, No. 39434/98, paras. 15-17, 31 mai 2005.

29 *Freedom and Democracy Party (OZDEP) v. Turkey*, para. 14; *Dicle pour le Parti de la démocratie (DEP) c. Turquie*, para. 22; *Yazar and others v. Turkey*, para. 22; *Emek Partisi et Senol c. Turquie*, para. 16; *Parti socialiste et autres c. Turquie*, para. 15; *Parti socialiste de Turquie (STP) et autres c. Turquie*, para. 18.

30 *United Communist Party of Turkey and Others v. Turkey*, para. 10.

Department of the government "on the ground that religious affairs should be under the control of the religious institutions themselves".[31]

The ECtHR responded to these dissolutions almost identically, finding in all of them a violation of Article 11 (2) of the Convention, which was of crucial importance to the further practice of the Constitutional Court of Turkey and of other European supreme/constitutional courts in this field. However, even before the ECtHR rendered its precedent (*United Communist Party of Tutkey*) at the end of January 1998, the Constitutional Court had already changed its approach in the given matter, in mid-January 1998, by dissolving the Welfare Party with due respect for ECtHR's balancing requirements. In this case the dissolution was based on the fact that the party had become "the center of activities against the principle of secularism", and was supported by a detailed analysis of the statements of the party leaders, its deputies and officers of the local government, as well as by a thorough analysis of the attitude of the Party towards all of them. Starting from the position that secularism is one of the premises for democracy, and that in Turkey this principle is particularly protected because of its specific historical experience and incompatibility of Sharia law and democracy, the Constitutional Court pointed out that the principle of secularism forbids the state to express its partiality towards a religion or a belief, and creates basis for the freedom of consciousness and equity of the citizens before the law.[32] Even if the result was the same – the Court's ruling in all the cases was positive – the militancy and illiberal reasoning were substituted by an overall examination of the Party's active and passive stance, in order to establish whether there was a pressing social need for such a radical measure.

This change in the Constitutional Court's approach can certainly be explained by the fact that the *Welfare Party* was the first case of a judicial dissolution of a political party which had won the biggest number of votes in the election and seats in *Meclis* (the Grand National Assembly of Turkey). This obliged the Court to explain its position in more detail, in order to legitimize it, and to have it better accepted by Turkish society.

Nevertheless, one should not disregard the influence of the Convention organs and their case law in this respect. In fact, even though the decision on the dissolution of the Welfare Party almost coincided with the ECtHR precedent in the *United Communist Party of Turkey*, which on its own excludes the possibility of direct influence, the existence of an indirect influence is undeniable. The reasoning in the *United Communist*

31 *Freedom and Democracy Party (OZDEP) v. Turkey*, para. 14.

32 *Refah Partisi (the Welfare Party) and Others v. Turkey*, Nos. 41340/98, 41342/98 and 41344/98, para. 25, 13 February 2003.

Party is mainly based on the opinion of the European Commission on Human Rights expressed in a public hearing before the ECtHR Grand Chamber, towards the end of 1997, in which representatives of the Turkish Government were also present.[33] On that occasion, the Commission took the position that "political parties should be able to campaign for a change in the law or the legal and constitutional structures of the State, provided of course that the means used for the purpose were in all respects lawful and democratic and that the proposed change was itself compatible with fundamental democratic principles".[34] Extending the reach of the *Handyside* judgment,[35] concerning the freedom of expression (Article 10 of the Convention), to the cases falling under Article 11,[36] the Commission concluded that the decision regarding the dissolution of a political party cannot lay exclusively on "information" and "ideas" in the party's program and constitution, no matter how "offensive", "shocking" or "disturbing" they are.[37] That the Constitutional Court of Turkey was aware of this "combined reading" of articles 10 and 11 of the Convention is also clear from the fact that the Constitutional Court judges who dissented in the *Welfare Party* case pointed out that that ruling was not compatible with provisions of the Convention and the practice of the ECtHR on dissolution of political parties, given that "political parties which do not support use of violence should have the possibility to participate in the political life and that in a pluralist system there must be space for debate on ideas considered upsetting, or even shocking".[38] Finally, even if the dissolution of the Welfare Party was decided on 16 January 1998, and the judgment of the ECtHR in the *United Communist Party* was rendered on 30 January 1998, the ruling of the Constitutional Court of Turkey was published in

33 *United Communist Party of Turkey and Others v. Turkey*, para. 6.

34 *Id.*, para. 50 (emphasis added).

35 *Handyside v. the United Kingdom*, No. 5493/72, 7 December 1976.

36 The structure and wording of Article 10 are very similar to that of Article 11: "1. Everyone has the right to freedom of expression. This right shall include freedom to hold opinions and to receive and impart information and ideas without interference by public authority and regardless of frontiers. This Article shall not prevent States from requiring the licensing of broadcasting, television or cinema enterprises.

2. The exercise of these freedoms, since it carries with it duties and responsibilities, may be subject to such formalities, conditions, restrictions or penalties as are prescribed by law and are necessary in a democratic society, in the interests of national security, territorial integrity or public safety, for the prevention of disorder or crime, for the protection of health or morals, for the protection of the reputation or rights of others, for preventing the disclosure of information received in confidence, or for maintaining the authority and impartiality of the judiciary".

37 *United Communist Party of Turkey and Others v. Turkey*, para. 50.

38 *Refah Partisi (the Welfare Party) and Others v. Turkey*, para. 43.

the Official Gazette on 22 February 1998,[39] which means that, while drafting the reasoning of its judgment, the Constitutional Court of Turkey had insight into the emerging Convention case-law.

3.2. Establishing the Convention Case-Law

The Turkish Constitutional Court dissolutions were condemned by the ECtHR, which found a violation of Article 11 (2) of the Convention in all of them, with the exception of dissolution of the Welfare Party.[40] Already in the first judgment from this series – *the United Communist Party of Turkey* – the ECtHR defined the guidelines of its case law in this field. The ECtHR started from the premise that "one of the principal characteristics of democracy [is] the possibility it offers of resolving a country's problems through dialogue, without recourse to violence, even when they are irksome", and that "democracy thrives on freedom of expression", as well as that "from that point of view, there can be no justification for hindering a political group solely because it seeks to debate in public the situation of part of the State's population and to take part in the nation's political life in order to find, according to democratic rules, solutions capable of satisfying everyone concerned".[41]

Having verified that in the concrete case the program of the Communist Party corresponded to the given objectives, the ECtHR did not exclude the possibility that the Party's program was hiding the objectives and intentions the Party had pled for, which, according to the Court, required a comparison of the Party's program with the actions of the party and its leaders and the positions they had defended, taken as a whole. Nevertheless, "in the present case, the TBKP's [United Communist Party of Turkey] program could hardly have been belied by any practical action it took, since it was dissolved", as the ECtHR noted, "immediately after being formed and accordingly did not even have time to take any action. It was thus penalized", according to the ECtHR, "for conduct relating solely to the exercise of freedom of expression".[42]

---

39 *Id.*, para. 44.

40 The ECtHR upheld that dissolution taking into account that in ruling on it the Constitutional Court had established that the restriction had been necessary in a democratic society.

41 *United Communist Party of Turkey and Others v. Turkey*, para. 57; *Freedom and Democracy Party (OZDEP) v. Turkey*, para. 44; *Parti socialiste et autres c. Turquie*, para. 50; *Yazar and others v. Turkey*, para. 48; *Dicle pour le Parti de la démocratie (DEP) c. Turquie*, para. 45; *Parti socialiste de Turquie (STP) et autres c. Turquie*, para. 46.

42 *United Communist Party of Turkey and Others v. Turkey*, para. 58. *See*, *mutatis mutandis*: *Freedom and Democracy Party (OZDEP) v. Turkey*, para. 42; *Parti socialiste et*

The ECtHR elaborated its principled position on the role of political parties in a democratic society and on conditions for the restriction of their actions in its next judgment, deciding on the dissolution of the Socialist Party. Relying on the thesis that democracy thrives on freedom of expression and that there is no justification for hindering a political group solely because it participates in the nation's political life, the ECtHR underlined that "it is the essence of democracy to allow diverse political programs to be proposed and debated, even those that call into question the way a State is currently organized, provided that they do not harm democracy itself".[43]

Ruling on the dissolution of the National Workers' Party, the ECtHR noted the conditions under which a political party can fight for a change of the legal system of the country: "Firstly, the means used to that end must in every respect be legal and democratic, and secondly, the change proposed must itself be compatible with fundamental democratic principles".[44] In other words, a "political party whose leaders incite to violence or put forward a policy which does not comply with one or more of the rules of democracy or which is aimed at the destruction of democracy and the flouting of the rights and freedoms recognized in a democracy cannot lay claim to the Convention's protection against penalties imposed on those grounds".[45]

When it comes to the identification of parties' actions with terrorist actions, based on the equivalence of the aims they fight for, the ECtHR pointed out that "if merely by advocating those principles a political group were held to be supporting acts of terrorism, that would reduce the possibility of dealing with related issues in the context of a democratic debate and would allow armed movements to monopolize support for the principles in question".[46]

The ECtHR concluded its 'Turkish case-law' on legitimacy of freedom of association restrictions with the *Welfare Party* judgment. Confronted with the application of a party which was in power at the moment of its dissolution, and which advocated radical changes of the Turkish legal system,

autres c. Turquie, para. 48; *Yazar and others v. Turkey*, para. 50; *Dicle pour le Parti de la démocratie (DEP) c. Turquie*, para. 47; *Parti socialiste de Turquie (STP) et autres c. Turquie*, para. 47-48.

43 *Parti socialiste et autres c. Turquie*, para. 47, *in fine*.

44 *Yazar and others v. Turkey*, para. 49.

45 *Id.*

46 *Yazar and others v. Turkey*, para. 57; *Dicle pour le Parti de la démocratie (DEP) c. Turquie*, para. 54; *Parti de la démocratie et de l'evolution et autres c. Turquie*, para. 25; *Emek Partisi et Senol c. Trquie*, para. 28.

announcing a possible use of force for the purpose of their achievement, the ECtHR had all the facts from which to elaborate at what moment the dissolution of a party was indeed "necessary in a democratic society", and, in particular, when was there a pressing social need for it. Considering that "a State cannot be required to wait, before intervening, until a political party has seized power and begun to take concrete steps to implement a policy incompatible with the standards of the Convention and democracy", the ECtHR established the conditions for the scrutiny of a "pressing social need". In the ECtHR's view, those conditions are:

> Whether there was plausible evidence that the risk to democracy, supposing it had been proved to exist, was sufficiently imminent; whether the acts and speeches of the leaders and members of the political party concerned were imputable to the party as a whole; and, whether the acts and speeches imputable to the political party formed a whole which gave a clear picture of a model of society conceived and advocated by the party which was incompatible with the concept of a "democratic society".[47]

3.3. *Reception of the Convention Case-Law*

The ECtHR reasoning in *Welfare Party*, and its case law on dissolution of political parties in general, had a significant impact on the practice of the supreme/constitutional courts in Europe. Even though the dissolution of another Turkish party – National Democratic Party (HADEP) – was not upheld by the ECtHR, the Turkish Constitutional Court had grounded its judgment on relations between HADEP and the PKK terrorist organization, in other words, on the party's actions, and not only on the statements of its leaders. The dissolution was principally argued by the incident, during HADEP's annual general meeting, in which the Turkish flag had been taken down and replaced with a PKK flag, and a poster of the then leader of the PKK, Abdullah Öcalan. Establishing the violation of Article 11 (2) of the Convention, the ECtHR particularly considered the fact that the person who had committed the incident had not been a member of HADEP, and that the HADEP's Congress publicly condemned the incident immediately after it had taken place, that it continued to dissociate itself from it and to condemn it as an attack on a common symbolic value of the people of Turkey.[48]

Besides the reorientation of the Turkish Constitutional Court, the change is present in the reasoning of the Constitutional Court of Germany.

---

47 *Refah Partisi (the Welfare Party) and Others v. Turkey*, para. 104.

48 *Hadep and Demir v. Turkey*, No. 28003/03, paras. 73 and 74, 14 December 2010, in relation to paras. 9, 13 and 15.

Only a month after the ECtHR Grand Chamber ruled in *Welfare Party*, the Federal Constitutional Court suspended the procedure for the dissolution of the National Democratic Party of Germany (*Nationaldemokratische Partei Deutschlands*) having established that the Federal Office for the Protection of the Constitution (*Verfassungsschutz*) – another instrument of militant democracy – had used secret investigators who, at the same time, had occupied high party offices, a fact which was not known either by the Constitutional Court or by the Party itself.[49] It follows that in a modern liberal democracy, a procedure that may lead to a serious limitation of fundamental rights, such as the dissolution of a political party, must respect the most stringent standards of the right to a fair trial, including the investigation preceding a trial and the gathering of evidence.[50]

The reception of the Convention case law may be observed also in the practice of the Spanish Supreme Court. In deciding on the necessity and the proportionality of dissolution of Herri Batasuna, a political wing of the terrorist organization ETA, the Supreme Court was guided by the ECtHR standards. Concluding that frequent calls to violence justify the measure of dissolution with the aim of protection of fundamental rights, the Supreme Court referred in particular to the *Welfare party* case, considering that "that judgment imposed on parties claiming to exercise functions in a democratic society a real legal duty to distance themselves from any ambiguous or unclear messages as to the use of violence". Furthermore, the Supreme Court pointed out that Batasuna's calls to violence appeared to be more explicit than those submitted to the ECtHR in *Welfare Party*.[51] Reasoning along similar lines, the Supreme Court ruled on a ban of another political party, Accion Nacionalista Vasca, acting also as a political wing of ETA.[52] Both bans were upheld by the ECtHR,

---

49 Фогел, Х.-Х., "Забрана политичких странака у Немачкој", у Б. Ненадић, Љ. Павловић (прир.), *Уставно ограничење слободе удруживања*, Уставни суд Републике Србије, Европска комисија за демократију путем права, Београд 2010, стр. 27-28. <Vogel, H.-H., Banning of Political Parties in Germany, B. Nenadić, Lj. Pavlović (ed.), *Constitutional Restriction of Freedom of Association*, Constitutional Court of the Republic of Serbia, European Commission for Democracy through Law, Belgrade, pp. 27-28>.

50 Brems, E., "Freedom of Political Association and the Question of Party Closures", in W. Sadurski (ed.), *Political Rights under Stress in 21st Century Europe*, Oxford University Press, Oxford, 2006, p. 189.

51 Ruling of the Spanish Supreme Court is cited according to its reference in the pertinent judgment of the ECtHR. *Herri Batasuna and Batasuna v. Spain*, Nos. 25803/04 and 25817/04, para. 38, 30 June 2009.

52 *Eusko Abertzale Ekintza – Acción Nacionalista Vasca (EAE-ANV) c. Espagne (No. 2)*, No. 40959/09, 15 janvier 2013.

which strongly relied in its judgments on the reasoning of the Spanish judiciary.

Finally, *Vona v. Hungary* concerned the decision of the Hungarian judiciary to dissolve an association whose activists, wearing military-looking uniforms, and applying military-like formations (imitating those of the World War II Hungarian Nazi movement – Arrow Cross), carried out several rallies, involving some 200 persons, in a village of approximately 1,800 inhabitants, including a Roma minority.[53] Finding that there was no violation of Article 11 (2) of the Convention, the ECtHR further refined its standing on when there is a pressing social need for the dissolution. It held, in particular, that if the right to freedom of assembly is repeatedly exercised by way of intimidating marches involving large groups, and related to the advocacy of racially motivated policies, incompatible with the fundamental values of democracy, the State is entitled to take measures restricting the freedom of association in so far as it is necessary to avert the danger which such large-scale intimidation represents for the functioning of democracy.[54]

4. Conclusion

In a decade and a half, starting with *United Communist Party of Turkey* (1998), through *Welfare Party* (2003) and *Herri Batasuna* (2009), to *Vona* (2013), the ECtHR fundamentally changed the European constitutional standards of freedom of association restrictions. It transformed the political party dissolution from an illiberal measure – the most important in the arsenal of militant democracy – into an essentially human rights institution. Central to this shift has been the praetorian introduction of a balancing test, enshrined formally in a "necessary in a democracy" principle. Thereby, one line of analysis, namely that the political party dissolution is permissible on the grounds of simple advocacy of major changes in the government's form, has been supplanted by another – a close scrutiny whether there is pressing social need for the given measure of human rights restriction, and whether it would be proportional.

It is self-evident that such a radical change in the judicial practice would not have been possible without the readiness of the national supreme/ constitutional courts to embrace and follow the Convention case law, sometimes in direct opposition to their national constitutional traditions. This is why the europeanization of constitutional standards of freedom of

53 *Vona v. Hungary*, No. 35943/10, paras. 64-65, 9 July, 2013.

54 *Id.*, para. 69.

association restrictions is also a story of judicial self-empowerment. As the constitutional pluralism thesis claims, there is no hierarchy between the foundational constitutional documents of the interacting national and supranational legal orders. In such heterarchical legal framework, key players, in the field of human rights protection, are the courts – international and national – which through a vertical and horizontal cooperation with each other and in relation to other institutional players determine the limits of their own powers.

States, People(s) and/or Constitution

The Core Problem of a European Rule of Law

Gérard RAULET

The glorification of "cosmopolitanism" in the dominant discourse ignores that the globalization process has very little to do with the situation which Kant described in his treaty *On Perpetual Peace.* It is even an inversion of it. Kant emphasized the *national state* for at least two reasons. Firstly because it was the level and space where the freedom of the individual could be realized as the sovereignty of the citizens, and secondly because an abstract "philanthropic" cosmopolitanism would ignore the anthropological and historical differences, the very different rhythms of evolution, and therefore also what is actually in question: *a rule of law*! As Habermas wrote, one has to be "critical of the liberal assumption that human rights are prior to popular sovereignty".[1] Habermas draws (implicitly) the lesson of Carl Schmitt who pointed out that Humanity is *not* a political concept. In another essay on "The Concept of human dignity and the realistic utopia of human rights", he observed that "the trick to the legal character of human rights is that they protect a human dignity which gets its contents of self-respect and social recognition from a particular status in space and time: the status of the democratic citizen."[2]

This is, as I have shown in former publications on this question, the reason why Kant refused to skip the stage of republican nation-states.[3] These alone can guarantee the transition from the subject to the free human being, and from the *ancien régime* to a new international order. This is also the reason why in his treaty only a "federation of free states" is possible and not immediately a worldwide republic. Any attempt to realize the World Republic prematurely would degenerate

1 Habermas, Jürgen, "Multiculturalism and the Liberal State", in *Stanford Law Review*, Vol. 47, No. 5 (May, 1995), p. 852.

2 Habermas, J., "Das Konzept der Menschenwürde und die realistische Utopie der Menschenrechte", in *Zur Verfassung Europas. Ein Essay*, Frankfurt am Main, Suhrkamp, 2011, p. 30.

3 See Raulet, Gérard, *Critical Cosmology. On Nations and Globalization: a philosophical essay*, Lanham, Lexington Books, 2005, Chapter two: "Citizenship, Otherness and Cosmopolitanism in Kant", pp. 25-34.

and regress to the claim of a Universal Monarchy which characterized the *ancien régime*. It should be remembered that the beginning of European publicities co-incided with an affirmation of nationalities. Whereas the nation-states of the Old Regime were in fact feudal multinationals, in 1789 and then in 1848 nationalities were associated with the awakening of political public opinion. The core of this Kantian conception is the constitutional moment. How does the problem look like in the globalized world order in which the role of the sovereign national state is undermined by the structural changes of the reproduction of the capital?

The Decline of the Social State and the Displacement of Borders

The national state must insure the link between global capitalism and the productive forces that feed into it but remain nonetheless national. It assumes, in the framework imposed upon European nations by the European Commission – an exemplary case of the rapport between the local (potentially ex-national) and the global – the role of *regulator of deregulation*. Furthermore, it reproduces this schema in its own interior "managing territory" polity by discharging itself onto the local and regional collective missions that arose from the social state and which this latter can no longer support. One could accumulate examples of dossiers in which, notably when the state's economic and political power is led (as is to be expected) into failure, it shrugs the blame off onto local collectives. Despairing of its cause, it is on the local echelon that it expects to maintain the social and national link. We are witnessing a decentralization of the social state.[4] The social state localizes the social and practices massive territorial sub-treatment. This process, however voluntarily it may have been undertaken, doubtless corresponds not really to a deliberate political choice but to a structural evolution. If the nation-state, the Welfare State, thus "delegates" its missions, it is because it is doubled by economic and, most of all, financial globalization and is no longer in the position to act both economically and politically. The problem is not only that the relationship of politics to the market has gotten out of balance on a global scale but that the national governments are powerless in establishing acceptable social standards. The active position lost to the nation state on the international scale is lost as well to the social state. Therefore it confides to local authorities the mission of managing globalization's

4 Cf. Garnier, Jean-Pierre, "Du spatial au social, du local au global", in Bidet, Jacques and Texier, Jacques (ed.), *Le nouveau système du monde*, pp. 125-150 – a masterful demonstration (and deconstruction) of this logic.

fallout, not only on the economic and social plane, but also on the plane of citizenship, which is to say on the infinitely more serious plane of its own legitimacy.

On the other hand nobody can deny the nationalist effects induced by the process of globalisation. We must also inscribe them in the process of de-legitimisation of nation states, first of all Welfare States, in the multiplication process of differentials and the displacement of borders, as much geopolitical as social, which it induces. Most of these nationalisms presented themselves as liberation-nationalisms and there is indeed no reason to distinguish between the Croatian or the Ukrainian emancipation on the one side and political "autonomies" (like in Spain or Great Britain – Scotland – for instance) in Western European states on the other side; in both cases, if we look closely, it is a matter of re-subdividing, by the formation of autonomic Republics and under cover of political emancipation, the inherited frame of constitutional sovereignty and economic reproduction. In quite a lot of cases it is also for the threatened national state a good opportunity of dropping the poorer regions. The lesson which can be drawn is, as Habermas writes, that the supposed "world society" is stratified and hierarchical and rests on "an asymmetrical interdependencies between developed nations, newly industrialized nations, and the less developed nations".[5]

Who Decides? Postnationalism and the Question of Sovereignty

Habermas' diagnosis of the withdrawal of the nation state has been widely misunderstood. In his book *The Postnational Constellation* (1998) he wrote already: "The phenomena of the territorial state, the nation, and a popular economy constituted within national borders formed a historical constellation in which the democratic process assumed a more or less convincing institutional form. [...] Wherever democracies on the Western model have appeared, they have done so in the form of the nation-state. Clearly, the nation-state fulfils important preconditions for societies constituted within determinate borders to exert a democratic form of self-control".[6] In other words, he acknowledged the decline of the nation state

5 Habermas, "Aus Katastrophen lernen? Ein zeitdiagnostischer Rückblick auf das kurze 20. Jahrhundert", in *Die postnationale Konstellation. Politische Essays*, Frankfurt/Main, Suhrkamp? 1998, p. 87. English translation: The *Postnational Constellation. Political Essays*, translated, edited and with an introduction by Max Pensky, Cambridge (Mas.), The MIT Press 2011, p. 54.

6 "Der Territorialstaat, die Nation und eine in nationalen Grenzen konstituierte Volkswirtschaft haben damals eine historische Konstellation gebildet, in der der demokratische Prozess eine mehr oder weniger überzeugende institutionelle Gestalt

but he did not at all give up its claims. As he stated in his essay of 2011 "Why Europe needs a Constitution" "the challenge before us is not to invent anything but to conserve the great democratic achievements of the European nation-state beyond its own limits".[7] The reason is that self determination can only exist when the people of the state (*Staatsvolk*) transforms itself "into a nation of citizens (*Staatsbürger*) who take their political destiny into their own hands".[8]

What Habermas calls the "post-national state", that is, a state which no longer draws its legitimacy from national history, from race, blood or soil, could better be characterized as "*post-nationalist*" insofar as the stage of the nation-state cannot be evaded. It still rests on the modern momentum of citizenship, that is, as Habermas has called it, on "constitutional patriotism" (*Verfassungspatriotismus*). Constitutional patriotism has, or rather should, become the basis of modern identity in the "post-traditional society".[9] As long as the "post-national" (or "post-nationalist") identity does not draw its legitimacy from a national history or a so-called national identity but from Society, it is then the "Nation" as Society in the sense already expressed by Sieyès. The other side of the medal is that this *modern* national identity tends then to perceive the state only as a manager and redistributor of wealth: for that reason the equation Society-Nation *must* engender values, and not only material values. This is precisely the function of publicity, the political equivalent of which is called citizenship in the French tradition and means nothing else than the "*republikanische Gesinnung*", the republican mentality discussed by Habermas.

Habermas reminds us that the nationalism which has developed in Europe since the end of the 18th century is a specifically modern form of collective identity which rested on a key concept emphasised by him: *solidarity*.[10] Solidarity is the Habermasian concept for

annehmen konnte. […] Wo immer Demokratien westlichen Zuschnitts entstanden sind, haben sie die Gestalt von Nationalstaaten angenommen. Der Nationalstaat erfüllt offensichtlich wichtige Erfolgsvoraussetzungen für die demokratische Selbststeuerung der Gesellschaft." (Habermas, "Die postnationale Konstellation und die Zukunft der Demokratie", in *Die postnationale Konstellation. Politische Essays*, *op. cit.*, p. 94 & p. 97); English translation, *op. cit.*, p. 60 & 62.

7 Habermas, "Why Europe needs a constitution", in *New Left Review*, 11 (Sept./Oct.), 2001, p. 6.

8 Habermas, "Die postnationale Konstellation und die Zukunft der Demokratie", in *Die postnationale Konstellation. Politische Essays*, p. 99; English translation, p. 64.

9 Habermas, "Geschichtsbewußtsein und posttraditionale Identität", in *Eine Art Schadensabwicklung*, Frankfurt am Main, Suhrkamp, 1987, pp. 161-162.

10 Habermas, "Die postnationale Konstellation und die Zukunft der Demokratie", in *Die postnationale Konstellation. Politische Essays*, *op. cit.*, p. 117: "In komplexen Gesellschaften bildet die in Prinzipien der Volkssouveränität und Menschenrechte

recognition. It means more or less the same as the French "fraternity". Compared with Honneth's one it has the advantage of including at once the constitutional problematics. In Habermas' view the issue of the "struggle for recognition" is the inclusion of all conflicting identities into the constitutional protection. In the context of the breakdown of the *ancien régime*, "it is that nationalism which provided an answer to the need for new identifications".[11] Nationalities were also associated with the awakening of political public opinion – of the "public sphere" (*Öffentlichkeit*). From these two points of view nationality was something progressive. Yesterday in the East, today in the Middle East, it seems that the awakening of nationalities or even religious identities are indispensable for recasting citizenship. This context certainly entails an enormous risk of regression, since traditional and premodern determinations – soil, language, religion, and even race – are reasserting themselves against universal, that is rational constitutional values. But this otherness is also at the heart of the matter concerning European identity. Let us hope that it can be mastered, because a European Union which ignores and represses national identities would also repress the formation of modern citizenship and would result, once again, in a Holy Alliance – the holy alliance of merely economic interests.

In his foreword to the collection of short essays on Europe which have been published in French in 2006, Habermas himself requested a referendum at the European level in its entirety. In the absence of such an act of adhesion to the finalities of the European construction, Europe, he wrote, can only be an "area of free trade growing in a diffuse fashion".[12] In other words the public opinion should be mobilised in order to "recapture" the deficit of legitimacy left by the laborious ratification of the treaty in 2005[13] and to "constitute a common political will which goes beyond national frontiers".

---

begründete deliberative Meinungs- und Willensbildung der Bürger letztlich das Medium für eine abstrakte und rechtsförmig hergestellte, über politische Teilnahme reproduzierte Form der Solidarität." English translation, p. 76.

11 *Ibid.*, p. 165.

12 Habermas, *Sur l'Europe*, Paris, Bayard, 2006, p. 6 (my translation: Habermas seems to have written this foreword for the French collection published by Christian Bouchindhomme).

13 It must be recalled that in June 2007 the "Treaty establishing a Constitution for Europe" was still ratified by only eighteen States out of twenty seven and that several others, in particular Poland and the United Kingdom, had announced they were no longer willing to carry on with the ratification process.

Mock Constitution, Artificial Citizenship

It is commonly argued that the European Community has already been transformed into a constitutional legal order, and that the arguments to the contrary are obsolete. Even in the case of a separate constitution some interprets argue that "a European constitution must [not] necessarily follow the format of constitutions commonly found in Nation States".[14] But constitutionalizing the Union is not just a technocratic step toward integration, it asks the question of *qualitatively different kinds of Union*. A constitutional legal order such as it is prefigured by the Charter of Rights of the EU and/or by the addition of the treaties is very different from a separate constitution cognisable as such. A treaty-by-treaty expansion of supranational jurisdiction into areas of public policy traditionally associated with the nation state cannot be considered as a real constitutionalizing process since it does not respect the basic idea of national democratic control and is therefore not able to compensate on one side the fact that the relationship of politics to the market has gotten out of balance and, on the other side, to overcome the completely legitimate tension between the accession to a mature transnational polity and the republican sense of sovereign self-determination.

The *proton pseudo* of the 2004 Constitution-Treaty – or, let us say in more diplomatic terms: its perplexingly hydrid sovereignty – consists in its invocation of the "citizens of Europe" in article 1. If citizenship does not pre-exist to the Constitution but is created by it (and this is the key of legitimacy), *it is necessary that the constitution constitutes*. The very title "Treaty establishing a Constitution for Europe" sums up the problem. On one hand, article I-6 unequivocally expresses that the Constitution goes beyond all prior treaties as the right of the Union must prevail over that of member-States. But on the other hand, article I-10 concedes that the Constitution is not really one as "Union citizenship is added to national citizenship but does not replace it". One can approve or, on the contrary, regret this duality; the fact is, however, that we are dealing with a "constitutional" construction which, as such, breaks free from the people's sovereignty and – this is the least that we can say – *does not respect its own principles* as expressed in the Charter of Fundamental Rights of the Union of 7 December 2000 (Preamble), repeated in Part II of the constitutional treaty: "[The Union] relies on the principle of democracy and that of the State of law." If, as Habermas has written, the citizens of the States of the Union "can have a founded interest for their own national State to

---

14 Craig, Paul, "Constitutions, Constitutionalism and the European Union", in *European Law Journal*, Vol. 7, No. 2, June 2001, p. 126.

keep playing the role of the keeper of right and liberty",[15] it is simply because this is their only constitutional guarantee *stricto sensu* – in the strict sense of the guarantee of a State of law.

As for the so-called European citizenship, it shows itself to be an abstraction since the "Treaty establishing a Constitution for Europe" does not supersede the decision of the 20 May 1998 French Constitutional Council: the European citizenship is in a sense "authorised" by the French constitution but in no way *founded* by it, nor by the "European Constitution".[16] In plain language: the Union does not have the competence to grant European citizenship; the granting of citizenship continues to be under the jurisdiction of national States, as stipulated by the Hague Convention of 12 April 1930 – long before institutional Europe took shape; the European Convention on Nationality of 6 November 1997 (art. 3, paragraph 1) only confirmed it. Therefore, there is not, to speak clearly, the slightest beginning of a true "European citizenship" in the full constitutional sense of the term. The nationals of the Union form a category of citizens of a particular kind, benefiting from a "special status" – according to the very formulation of the Protocol on asylum added as an annex to the 2 October 1997 Treaty of Amsterdam. However, in France as in Germany, foreigners remain excluded from exercising political rights.

Of course, the point of view of the lawyers cannot be ignored. Obviously, the existence of the European Court of Justice has done a lot to give the Union the character of a constitutional legal order and to make it different from a mere international treaty. The European Court of Justice possesses a judicial *Kompetenz-Kompetenz*.[17] The decisions of the European Court concern directly the peoples of Europe through and despite the legislations of the member states whose courts are bound to apply them. The supremacy and pre-emption of the Court's jurisprudence has been a key element in this evolution. The supporters of the "Transformation Thesis" argue therefore that the EU is no longer dependent on international law nor on the legal systems of the member states,

---

15 "Die Unionsbürger können […] ein begründetes Interesse daran haben, dass der jeweils eigene Nationalstaat auch in der Rolle eines Mitgliedstaates weiterhin die bewährte Rolle eines Garanten von Recht und Freiheit spielt." ("Die Krise der Europäischen Union im Lichte einer Konstitutionalisierung des Völkerrechts", in *Zur Verfassung Europas*, *op. cit.*, p. 72).

16 "The [French] Constitution only admits *the possibility of its existence*" (Haquet, Arnaud, *Le Concept de Souveraineté en Droit Constitutionnel Français*, Paris, PUF, 2004, p. 170).

17 Cf. for example Shilling, T., "The Autonomy of the Community Legal Order – An Analysis of Possible Foundations", in *Harvard International Law Journal*, 1996, 37. More literature in Craig, P., *op. cit.*, p. 134, note 53.

but that the constitutional treaty is *self-validating* since the EU has been changed from a legal relationship binding upon the states (which was already the case in the EEC) to an integrated legal order in which the controls on the exercise of public power are similar in nature to those found in nation states. *It is not the case, for quite a lot of reasons.*

Although its official purpose was to increase the power of the citizens (through the possibility of public initiative and through the extension of the legislative power of the parliament) the constitutional treaty of 2004 has not changed anything in the competencies and relationship of the European institutions. The confusion between the legislative and the executive power annihilates the extension of the citizens' sovereignty. The treaty attributes the legislative power to the Parliament and to the Council of Ministers which is composed of members of the executive of the member states (Art. I-20 & 23). Moreover, the Commission – which is not elected – has alone the power of proposing regulatory texts (Art. I-26). One must add that decision-making within the Council is by qualified majority and not unanimity. Dieter Grimm is perfectly right when he argues that public power in the EU is "not one that derives from the people, but one mediated through the states".[18]

In Laeken (Belgium) the European Council had incited the 105 writers of the treaty to-be to make the sharing of competencies between the supranational level of the Union and the intergovernmental level more transparent. They have distinguished a so-called "exclusive competency" belonging to the Union (which is to be found in Art. I-13) and shared competencies (Art. I-14) which are the most numerous. In this last case the states are allowed to legislate as long as the question has not been referred to the Union. This leads to the consequence that the Union can at every time take possession of a subject, which may be considered as contradictory with the principle of subsidiarity, and that it does it fast always in a liberalistic sense. A core question concerns the three pillars of the sustainable development: the economic, the social and the environmental constituents which are mentioned in the Lisbon text but are devolved to the Union as to the economy (Art. I-13), whereas the social and environmental questions are shared competencies (Art. I-14). This repartition prevents the member states from preferring another economic policy than the Union (a very crucial point in the present context of the management of the "crisis"), and it prevents the Union from taking social or environmental regulations which are refused by the member states (which is less the case since the Union as a whole is much more neoliberal than several

18 Grimm, Dieter, "Does Europe Need a Constitution", in *European Law Journal*, 1995, 1, p. 291.

member states like France). A further example is the progressive implementation of a common defence policy. In Art. I-141 two references to the NATO without any clarification of the relative roles of the Union and the NATO make this important perspective of an increased supranational sovereignty completely unclear.

In as far as the constitutional treaty has invested the Union with a legal personality in order to enable it to sign treaties and to be represented as a whole in international organizations such as the WTO it is more than ever urgent to give to the citizens a direct power of influence on the legislative level and on the control of the executive power. Contrary to its ambition to possess a double legitimacy – that of intergovernmental treaties and that of the citizens' rights to participation and representation – the European Union suffers from a "contradiction within its constitution between a *legal text* and an organization that is *already* partially democratic on the one hand, and a form of domination whose *legal standard* is *still* largely non democratic on the other".[19]

Post-State Constitutionalism

The problem is for all that the question as to why constitutions have, and continue to have, legitimacy and authority. We can nevertheless put aside the view that such a democratic requirement implies necessarily a super state or at least a strong federation.[20] But if the constitutional treaty is a mock constitution for legal reasons it must be asked at which conditions it could be transformed in something else than an artificial democracy. This is the question asked by the critical thinkers of the "no demos thesis" and most notably by Dieter Grimm whose arguments have been discussed and partially taken over by Habermas.[21] But one must put correctly the accents: Habermas does not actually clamour for a constitution in the full sense of the term, he gives rather the priority to the formation of a European people which would be sufficiently homogeneous to form a democratic will. For this is also a way by which the European peoples would attribute the political sovereignty to themselves – provided that the

19 Brunkhorst, Hauke, "Demokratie in der globalen Rechtsgenossenschaft. Einige Überlegungen zur post-staatlichen Verfassung der Weltgesellschaft", in *Zeitschrift für Soziologie*, Sonderheft Weltgesellschaft, 2005, p. 22.

20 See Craig, pp. 138-9 where he refers to the position of Dieter Grimm: "There is no reason why such a constitution should inevitably lead to a European state. It would be perfectly possible for a constitution formulated from this foundation to accord sharply defined competences to the EU, and to enshrine protections for states' rights."

21 Habermas, "Remarks on Dieter Grimm's 'Does Europe Need a Constitution'", in *European Law Journal*, 1995, 1.

European institutions, as we have described them, be changed in order to take this democratic will into account.[22] Have we any reason to hope this?

Even though constitutionalism has become a very encumbering procedure the question is whether it is possible to disconnect legitimacy from constitutionalism and what such a legitimacy would look like. As we have seen Habermas hopes that a referendum could initiate a political community which is not State controlled. In his 2004 text "Europeans, one last effort!"[23] Habermas contested "the idea that Europe cannot endow itself with a constitution because it has no constituting 'subjects'".[24] Thus, he somewhat took the defence of the constitutional treaty in its ideal form, that is as it should have been thought out, without the contradictions which we have pointed out above. Yet now, as Article 1, paragraph 1 of the Treaty refers to both citizens and States, or their peoples, he suggests that we should rather consider *peoples* as "the other constituting subject".[25] In doing so he *reintroduces a substantialist conception of the people or the nation in a debate that should only cover "constitutional patriotism"*. This is the reason why the question of knowing if the citizens of the Union only become citizens by concluding the Union, or if they originally are, is not trivial. It seems to me that there is here a very striking contradiction between the plea for a European constitution (and not only for a constitutional spirit or *Gesinnung*) which Habermas published in 2001 in the *New Left Review*[26] and the idea that there may be "other" ways of grounding the European identity, in other words: other constituting subjects than the subject which is itself constituted as subject through the constitution. Thus the question is if essentialist (or substantialist) notions of identity are accepted and

---

22 Paul Craig gives an overview of the legal difficulties of the creation of a European constitution on p. 139-150. He underlines not less than 10 points some of which I sum up here with my own comments: (a) The allocation of power between EU institutions (this is the main problem which I have aimed at here), (b) The nature of the constitutional document: abstraction vs. detail (the question as to why it should only consist in a few abstract principles – which is more or less the present situation that leaves the lobbies, the states and the Commission itself completely free to politicize the decisions in their sense – see again the description above), (c) The place of the Charter of Rights within the constitutional scheme, (d) The question of the community policies that should be included within a constitution, (e) The allocation of competence between the EU and the member states (see above), (f) The definition of the relationship between the EU and the member states, (g) The formal status of a Constitution. Etc.

23 German original: "Ein Ruck muss durch *Europa* gehen", in *Die Weltwoche*, No. 21, 19 May 2004.

24 *Ibid.*

25 "als das andere Subjekt der Verfassungsgebung" ("Die Krise der Europäischen Union im Lichte einer Konstitutionalisierung des Völkerrechts", *op. cit.*, p. 67).

26 Habermas, "Why Europe needs a constitution", in *New Left Review*, 11 (Sept./Oct.), 2001, pp. 5-26.

may provide the grounding of the European identity. Habermas himself has summed up the problem in the following manner: "The controversial issue is briefly the following: Should citizen's identities as members of ethnic, cultural, or religious groups *publicly* matter, and if so, how can collective identities make a difference between the frame of constitutional democracy?"[27] If the answer is that private and cultural group identities publicly matter, then the consequence is a regression to the same confusion as in the "romantic nationalism" which Habermas rightly combats: a way of life – either that of the nation-constituting majority or that of a minority – imposes itself as the expression of the common inner life, or it tries to do so and the only escape seems to be multiculturalism. This can only be overcome if universal normative claims transcend the different lifeworlds and the claims of particular or collective life. In his essay on "The Postnational Constellation" Habermas applied himself to work out the difference between a "prepolitical" understanding of the nation as a "community of destiny"[28] (*Schicksalsgemeinschaft*) and he took the example of the "Germanists" of the failed German constitutional revolution of 1848 in order to define what can be called "*ein Volk*".[29] He underlined "the past oriented idea of a *Volksgeist* which put the future oriented claims of the liberals in difficulty".[30]

It is therefore surprising that Habermas' concept of People(s) seems to exist prior to the constitutional act which, all at once, constitutes the State and elevates the citizen to a realisation of the potentiality of citizenship, by making him the constituting subject. Habermas follows the German Federal Constitutional Court's comment on the Maastricht treaty according to which a "demos" is the political expression of a people whose prior definition is given by organic-cultural features. Such "demoi" in the EU are found severally. The problem is the relationship between a formal definition of People as statehood and a substantive condition of this statehood, that is if the "demos" is the political manifestation of a people already existing as a collective entity and identity on organic-cultural basis. Whilst this definition takes the ethnic or cultural "demos" out of constitutionalism we should at this point remember Sieyès whose concept of Nation is, on the contrary, inseparable from a domination constituting act (in German: *Herrschaftsbegründung*) which, correctly understood, has been achieved in two steps (which are mostly merged): the *Etats*

27 Habermas, "Multiculturalism and the Liberal State. Address", in *Stanford Law Review*, 47/5, p. 849.

28 Habermas, *Die postnationale Konstellation*, *op. cit.*, p. 117.

29 *Ibid.*, p. 13-46.

30 *Ibid.*, p. 17.

généraux and the *Assemblée nationale*. The first step was a *tabula rasa*: it began with the evidence that there is a part of the society which is not represented and which even counts for nothing although it is a constitutive component of the Christian order. Sieyès expressed that through the famous syllogism: "Qu'est-ce que le Tiers-Etat? Tout. Qu'a-t-il été jusqu'à présent dans l'ordre politique? Rien. Que demande-t-il? A être quelque chose." What he claimed was a sort of universality *ex negativo* which he imposed through the second step when he asked the other estates to renounce their privileges[31] in order to build this new community which had never existed before: the Nation. He did not call only to any Right of Nature or to Human Rights – and this is the very difference between his constitutional act and the European quasi-constitution – because a mere protest against injustice would not have been enough in order to subvert radically the established Christian order. The Nation had to be something completely new – this was the step leading from the *Etats généraux* to the totally new concept of an assemblée nationale on the 17th of June 1789: "*Le Tiers seul, dira-t-on, ne peut pas former les Etats généraux. Eh! Tant mieux! Il composera une Assemblée nationale.*"[32]

In opposition to that Habermas – and some of his followers – seem to have only the choice between a premodern and substantial concept of the People which goes along with the growing delegitimization of the republican nation state and, on the other hand, supranational institutions which, as Habermas quite lucidly notes, are merely "*herrschaftsbegrenzend*" – power limitating – and which remind of premodern models.[33] This is not only the case on the level of the international right, where they serve only to "preserve the balance between the 'dominant powers'"[34] (as it was the case in the pre-modern order criticized by Kant at the end of his essay on "Theory and Practice" – for instance in the "Project of a Perpetual Peace" of Abbé de Saint-Pierre) but also on the level of the citizen's rights in as far as the supranational organizations – even the EU – are not able to ensure the social rights which are not separable from the "domination grounding" constitution of the republican rule of law. The main trend is much more that at this supranational level the social rights and the rights of the citizens are sacrificed.

31 "en se purgeant de leurs injustes privilèges" (Sieyès, *Qu'est-ce que le Tiers-Etat?*, Paris, 1988, p. 154).

32 *Ibid.*, p. 155.

33 "die supranationalen Verfassungen [erinnern] in ihrer herrschaftsbegrenzenden Funktion an Vorbilder einer vormodernen Tradition" (Habermas, "Hat die Konstitutionalisierung des Völkerrechts noch eine Chance?", in *Der gespaltene Westen*, Frankfurt am Main, Suhrkamp, 2004, p. 136).

34 Habermas, *ibid.*, pp. 136-7.

What is vanishing is nothing less than the idea of legitimation. This tendency cannot be hold back by the fantastic idea of a World civil society which only exists as the weak public sphere of the web or of the NGOs, that is in the form of organizations which can certainly put some pressure on the governments, but they are, as their name clearly says, *non-governmental*: in other words, they may protest and propose but they do not participate in the legislative power, their influence is not different from that of the lobbies against which they fight. To the same extent as the inherited concept of representation through institutionalized parties is facing a preoccupying crisis the weak constitutionalism in which Habermas and other thinkers see the premises of a supranational legitimacy proves to be only the flip side of a weak republican public sphere. The civic deliberations concerning pressing questions may get loose from the political structures of the state but their implementation requires the other two constitutive processes of democracy: participation and voting. Modern collective identity can emerge from a public debate concerning common aims and different ideas of the good, that is from specific cultural resources – from different lifeworlds. *But legally mediated solidarity* springs exclusively from democratic citizenship. If, as Habermas emphasizes it, the key question is to expand civil solidarity transnationally across Europe, then even a "European-wide public sphere" will not be enough: the core problem is a democratic constitutional framework, a European rule of law. The "democratic deficit" about which the current discourse on the EU complains is not at all a mere "portmanteau". It does not only imply informational and cognitive deficits *but a structural problem of sovereignty*.

Remarks on the Normative Understanding of a Transnational European Democracy

Alexandre DUPEYRIX

If we try to grasp the meaning of the European project and to define its *purpose* today (its *finalité*), four different approaches are possible:[1]

– the first approach, a negative one: democracy is a matter of sovereignty, and the nation state is the only framework where sovereignty can develop and express itself. By contrast, the European Union (EU) represents negatively the disintegration of the nation state and of national identities, and hence the decline of sovereignty and democratic citizenship; for such Euro-sceptical observers, state and sovereignty are the essence of politics; therefore they consider the "post-national" as post-political and post-democratic;

– others advocate the view that the aim of the process of European integration is a federal state. At the beginning of the European construction, they used to refer to the American model and to speak of the United States of Europe (representing the pacifist utopia of the post-First World War period). This approach is in some sense the opposite of the previous position, but both think in terms of a state. Their conception of a supranational order is literally *super national*: they defend a super-state. This approach is perfectly legitimate, however it encounters huge historical and empirical difficulties which seem to prove Kant right when he wrote in his *Treaty of Perpetual Peace* that which seems accepted in *thesi* is rejected by the peoples of Europe in *hypothesi*: a supranational state is perhaps the *logical* and *rational* horizon of European integration but the people of Europe do not want to give up their national specificities and sovereignty;[2]

---

1 See Ferry, Jean-Marc, *La république crépusculaire*, Paris, Le Cerf, 2010.

2 Kant, Immanuel, *Zum ewigen Frieden*, Zweiter Abschnitt, welcher die Definitivartikel zum ewigen Frieden unter Staaten enthält, in Werke, hrsg. v. Weischedel, Frankfurt/Main, Insel, 1964, Bd. IX, pp. 203-213.

- others consider the above views outmoded and too restrictive respectively. They defend a minimalist and liberal conception of European integration: the EU is above all a common market, a free-trade area, where political and social consensus has just to be found on some general rules of fairness. Right-wing observers will suggest that this encourages innovation, attracts investment, creates wealth and economic growth, enables European citizens to eat cheap Spanish strawberries during the winter, to buy cheap cars built by Renault in Romania, to travel on low-cost airline companies to Greece for the weekend; left-wing commentators will insist that the common market has so far caused fiscal and social dumping, that the liberal idea that wealth created will "trickle down" from the top to the bottom of the society has proved wrong, and that Spanish strawberries simply have no taste;
- the fourth approach points out the *historical* and *processual* dimension of European integration. Observers defending this view believe the actual process of constitutionalization of the European legal order is triggered by economic and political challenges. They believe that politics and especially democracy must catch up with the economy. This would indeed be *the purpose of and the justification for the EU: to preserve democracy in a global age, beyond the borders of the nation state* (but also, by after-effects, within these borders, within the nation state), just as the founding of the nation state once aimed to stabilize a society challenged by the development of capitalism and demands for democratic self-legislation. This is the view advocated by Jürgen Habermas in recent articles,[3] although he used to defend, ten years ago, the model of a federal state. This is also the position defended by a great Habermas expert in France, Jean-Marc Ferry, whose work inspired this paper.[4]

Ferry develops the idea of "transnational" European integration and citizenship. This is not exactly the same as "supranational", nor "postnational", integration: the "supranational" transposes the characteristics of the nation state to the European level and remains caught in national patterns, whereas the "postnational" suggests that we say farewell to the nation state and that we could get rid of the national level just like that: which Habermas and Ferry do not consider desirable. By contrast,

3 See e.g. Habermas, Jürgen, *Zur Verfassung Europas*, Berlin, Suhrkamp, 2011.

4 See among others: Ferry, Jean-Marc, *L'éthique reconstructive*, Paris, Le Cerf, 1996; *La question de l'Etat européen*, Paris, Gallimard, 2000; *Europe, la voie kantienne*, Paris, Le Cerf, 2005; *La république crépusculaire*, Paris, Le Cerf, 2010.

"transnational" suggests horizontal, rather than vertical, integration. Like it or not, this transnational order may be the only option in order to face the overwhelming globalization process while maintaining democratic claims and requirements.

In this paper I would like to address the normative grounds of the EU from a philosophical point of view. "Normative" does not mean to answer to the question how or what the EU should be, but rather to ask how we might understand or interpret the evolution of the European project in order to perceive emerging norms – and to enhance, in a second step, relevant institutional innovations. It seems today that these norms or tendencies lean in the direction of a *transnational democracy*. In Parts I and II, I will discuss two major conceptual obstacles that must however be overcome if we wish to conceive a transnational democracy: *national identities* and *national sovereignties*. In Part III, I will sketch the transnational order that is being implemented.

The Issue of European Identity

A major obstacle to further European integration seems to be the absence of a genuine European identity. If there is no identity, there is no people – no "demos"; if there is no people, there is no political subject and therefore no *pouvoir constituant*, no citizenship, no democracy. I believe we can address the idea of identity by examining two types of oppositions: 1) substantial vs. processual identity; 2) cultural vs. political identity.

Substance vs. process. The first antithesis consists of understanding identity either as a *substance* or as a *process*. In the first case, *identity as substance*, the main features, the main characteristics of the concerned entity, are described by referring to a common history, a common culture (language, religion, traditions, rules of law, institutions), a common territory. This approach is usually accompanied by *constructivist* trends, inasmuch as defining characteristics means constructing a portrait, making choices, retaining features at the expense of others, following more or less unconscious strategies. As we know, the development of national identities in the 19th century involved political instrumentalization, glorification of the past, the creation of unifying myths and heroes – a national culture mainly passed on at school and passed on in families from one generation to another. In fact, the way we practice history sheds more light on our present than on our past. Anyway, this constructivism, despite its possible excesses, seems to be necessary and to fill a human psychological and cognitive need for concrete identification, as well as feeding an emotional sense of belonging: we need faces, we need names, we need stories, we need references, symbols, flags, colours, shapes.

There are many attempts, today in Europe, by intellectuals, journalists, writers, to give substance to the idea of Europe and to compensate seemingly distant and disembodied European institutions by writing a new history of Europe. The paradoxical result is that numerous *narratives* on the topic "Europe" and "European identity" are currently generated in the public sphere (not only in the academic sphere), narratives that do not necessarily overlap each other, that are even sometimes contradictory. Let me mention just two frequent examples:

- about the question of the religious roots of Europe: there are as many narratives arguing that Europe is above all a Christian continent as narratives showing that Islam is an essential part of our heritage. Other narratives will even emphasize that the most peculiar contribution of Europe to world history is the invention of secularism;
- concerning the geographical and territorial definition of Europe – a never ending discussion: there will be as many narratives including Turkey as excluding it – same thing with the ex-Russian republics, such as Ukraine or Georgia.

So the drawback of a substantial definition of identity is that we may never come to an agreement, to a consensus about what it means to be a European, or what Europe is and what it was, and what priority we are to give to each of the features discovered. But this should not make us particularly sceptical about the possibility of a European identity – and citizenship. We just have to realize that the issue is exactly the same at the nation state level. The French need only recall a recent public debate initiated by the French government in 2009-2010. A debate about "national identity" was staged, supposedly in order to answer such questions as: "what is France? What does it mean to be French?" This debate took place in each "prefecture", that is in each administrative district throughout the French territory – and the debates took also place of course in the public sphere and on the internet. The result was predictable: it was a complete shambles, in which no relevant contribution was audible, each individual was more French than his or her neighbour, chauvinistic, racist and islamophobic comments received the most attention, whereas people who might have said interesting things preferred to boycott this debate because of the obvious underlying political instrumentalization. The debate nevertheless had the virtue of providing empirical evidence that, while it may be legitimate to question one's identity, there cannot be a unique and homogeneous answer in a modern democracy, but only *multiple narratives*. In fact, a democratic space is precisely the space where everyone has the right to develop his or her own identity. And no institution can prescribe these.

In contrast to this substantial understanding, we can define identity as a *process* in *practical* and *pragmatic* terms. What really matters is not who or what we are, but *what we want to do.* Identity develops while we are acting, experiencing, cooperating, are confronted with success or failure. It is a *processual* definition turned toward the future, and not a substantial one looking back to the past. For instance: what matters is not so much the content or the results of the history of Europe historians and philosophers are currently writing, as the fact that they are writing it – and that *they want* to write it. This will, this acceptance, this incentive is the expression, the outward sign of this common identity understood in a processual way as an act, as a work in progress. This identity is an open identity that proves itself in a constant movement of pragmatic self-definition and self-experiencing. Concerning the European identity, the most important concern is therefore, *knowing more or less who we are, so as to decide what we want to do.*

Cultural vs. political identity. The second antithesis that can be useful to address the concept of identity consists of opposing a cultural and a political identity. In this respect we should admit that the European identity is a political identity – and not a cultural one – based on common political projects and constitutional principles of democracy. The only precondition is to subscribe to these principles – irrespective of our languages, religions or national histories. To feel a sense of belonging to a region, a country, specific traditions is not incompatible with the support of a political project. The (more or less substantial and cultural) identity of an individual is not the same thing as the political identity of a citizen. In fact, this political identity is characteristic of every citizen in a modern democracy (and not only of the EU) and refers on the one hand once again to the will to subscribe to common constitutional principles and on the other hand to the willingness to recognize *persons we do not know* as full and equal members of the same legal and political community (which is somehow the opposite of a cultural community that tries to define itself by substantial features and to found solidarity on proximity: shared values and traditions, same life experiences).

Yet, even if these antitheses (substance vs. process, cultural vs. political identity) are indeed helpful in trying to understand which sense of belonging is at stake in a European identity, one cannot dissociate so easily these different aspects from each other: acting together and going in the same direction (process) inevitably implies sharing at least a few values and referring roughly to a common history (substance); subscribing to constitutional principles (political identity) necessarily implies anchoring these principles in similar worldviews (cultural identity). So we probably have to find the right balance between a constructivist approach to identity and a pragmatic one, between a cultural definition and a political one. Among the attempts to give a slightly substantial definition of Europe, I would like to mention the works written by Jean-Marc Ferry. Even if we interpret identity as a work in progress, we cannot avoid trying to determine the main features that define our European culture and thinking about the prerequisites to a common identity. Ferry gives three elements of definition of a European identity:

First of all, he points to what could be regarded as the ethical basis of this identity: he calls it "a reconstructive ethics". This ethics has something to do with a recognition ethics and the fact that we cannot fully live our lives if we do not enjoy a complete respect of our dignity as moral agents. Dealing with collective entities, Ferry situates this recognition in the relationships between nation states or even within nation states between mainstream cultures and minorities: the recognition concerns recognition of past damages caused by a nation or a people to another – mostly in times of war. The high number of public acts of contrition or public demands for forgiveness over the last decades, and especially in the 1990s, between different European countries, but also involving Japan or South Africa, or from Western countries toward their ex-colonies, are the sign of a democratic will for reconciliation. It is democratic because it implies a self-reflexive, self-critical and decentred relationship with oneself and one's history, the consciousness that others have suffered and that they need a gesture of contrition to heal the injuries still present in their collective narratives. It is not about repentance and guilt, it is about responsibility. Thanks to these public demands for forgiveness and public reconciliations, what was destroyed is reconstructed, feelings of distrust and revenge give way to reciprocal recognition of equal dignity.[5]

According to Ferry, this reconstructive ethics, grounded in shared memories, is the basis for a *European constitutional patriotism*. As is well known, Jürgen Habermas deals with this topic during the *Historikerstreit* in the 1980s. In an article called "Geschichtsbewusstsein und posttraditionale Identität",[6] he draws a parallel between the self-reflexive construction of the individual identity and the self-critical construction of a national identity. To this end he refers to Kierkegaard and explains that Kierkegaard developed a "posttraditional" and "postconventional" conception of identity: the Kierkegaardian individual becomes him/herself by accepting the determinisms that have constituted it, by paradoxically

5 Ferry, J.-M., *L'éthique reconstructive*, *op. cit.*; *La question de l'Etat européen*, *op. cit.*, pp. 145-161.

6 Habermas, J., "Geschichtsbewusstsein und posttraditionale Identität", in *Eine Art Schadensabwicklung*, Frankfurt/Main, Suhrkamp, 1987.

choosing him/herself as a product of different determinisms. Thanks to this acceptance, to this self-appropriation, the individual takes up the threads of his/her life and assumes responsibility for what it is. That is properly the existential basis of a postconventional identity. Habermas demands the same kind of self-reflexive relationship to our collective and historical past: no denial, no undue glorification, but a reflexive re-appropriation of one's own traditions, the best as well as the worst. In the context of the *Historikerstreit*, Habermas then wrote that the shared conscience and memory of what happened in Auschwitz should be the cement of a European democratic collective identity. Jean-Marc Ferry, basically, adopts and generalizes this gesture of assumed responsibility (though he does not focus on genocide) and suggests that this reconstructive ethics should be the criterion of the willingness of nation states to enter into a democratic community of interests. This could be the normative point of view from which the EU might justify a temporary refusal of Turkey's EU accession, as long as the Turkish government does not recognize the Kurdish genocide – this point of view would be more relevant than geographical, cultural or religious arguments.

Besides this ethics operating in international relations, and especially in Europe, Ferry tries to highlight values or principles typical to the European culture. To this end, he develops the idea of a common grounding, a common civilizational basis constituted from the 16th to the 18th century; he identifies three founding moments:[7]

- the development of principles of *civility* in the 16th century (a subject philosophically broached by Erasmus and his *De civitate* (1530): civility is the ability to respect the different sensibilities encountered in the social life;
- then principles of *legality* developed especially in the 17th century: legality refers to the discipline of the political power that accepts to submit to the constitutional principles (the philosophical reference is here John Locke's *Two Treaties of the Government* from 1690);
- the third principle is the principle of *publicity* (illustrated by the concept of *Öffentlichkeit* developed by Immanuel Kant in 1795): publicity means that the political power becomes opened to criticism and recognizes the need for legitimization expressed by the citizens.

From these three principles (civility, legality, publicity) have resulted four kinds of values that are still constitutive today of our understanding of citizenship: values of *integrity*, *participation*, *solidarity* and

[7] Ferry, J.-M., *De la civilisation. Civilité, Légalité, Publicité*, Paris, Le Cerf, 2001.

personality (or self-accomplishment). According to Ferry, the specificity of the European Union lies in the fact that it has managed to transpose to the relationships between member-states these values originally attached to the relationships between citizens. The value of integrity (that led in internal law to the implementation of civil rights) corresponds to international law rules regulating the relationships between member-states; the value of participation (that led to civic rights) corresponds to the principles of cooperation between member-states; the value of solidarity (that led to social rights) is transposed to the level of the European regions where redistribution takes place according to an equalization principle between rich and less rich; and finally the value of self-accomplishment (that resulted in moral and cultural rights) corresponds to the principle of mutual recognition of cultural identities and minorities, sanctioned by the different European treaties.

Therefore, Europe not only possesses a strong and shared political culture, but it has also managed to transpose these common civilizational principles to the functioning of the Union.

However, and it is the third point stressed by Ferry, to develop and grow and stay lively, this political culture – as well as the European cultural as a whole – must be supported by a *dynamic European public sphere*. This public sphere comprehends both the political and the media public spheres:[8]

- the political public sphere depends on the will and the ability of politicians to broach subjects concerning Europe and to contribute to the formation of the political opinion and will of European citizens, instead of sinking into demagoguery. This pedagogic duty for which political parties are liable is even written in the German constitution (art. 21 / Grundgesetz). The dynamism of the European public sphere depends also on structural possibilities, that is on interconnections, both horizontal and vertical, between regional, national and European Parliaments.
- concerning the media public sphere, it is up to the different actors to put Europe on the agenda. If they do not, then they have a part of responsibility in the relative disinterest of the citizens for the European project and the lacking sense of European belonging.

Tied up with the problem of identity is the problem of *diversity*. Europeans seem to be confronted with an insurmountable challenge: how can they conciliate different cultures with each other? Different social habits?

---

8 See Habermas, J., "Hat die Demokratie noch eine epistemische Dimension?", in *Ach, Europa*, Frankfurt/Main, Suhrkamp, 2008.

Different political traditions? This irreducible pluralism concerns not only specific regional or national specificities like blue cheese, corrida or speed limits on highways; it concerns more generally and more deeply different conceptions of political justice, that is, the normative core of modern democracy. The constitutional patriotism might reduce this pluralism by referring to the smallest common denominator: the problem is precisely that these constitutional principles are differently interpreted according to each tradition. Therefore legislation on prostitution, drugs, euthanasia, different conceptions of secularism, the existence or not of a minimum wage, are not only contingent and anecdotic differences, they originate in diverse understandings of fundamental rights, whether we summarize them under the French triptych "liberté, égalité, fraternité" or under John Rawls' principles of justice.

I do not know if we will succeed in merging our different interpretations – nor do I know if such convergence is desirable; but I think that only the long-term effects of public discussion can bring about this convergence – sometimes also accelerated by crises. Public discussion cannot, in a short term, solve the different social and political problems, it cannot solve conflicts; it is like a slow infusion. We must not regard the public sphere in an anachronistic way as the antique agora; we should consider it in the long term of deliberative practices.[9] By use of *public reason*, we can confront different reasonable worldviews.

Undoubtedly, belonging to the Union and the existence of public debates will gradually modify our political cultures.

As concluding remarks to this first part, I would say that:

- a postnational identity is conceptually and empirically possible. And it is not incompatible with a national identity;
- we should not oppose a patriotic and emotional identity based on national patterns and a more intellectual, ethical identity that might develop on a supranational scale. This erroneous distinction results from a misunderstanding of what "constitutional patriotism" really is. The concept of "postconventional identity" developed by Habermas, must not be mistaken for the concept of "postnational". "Postconventional" can be relevant and operative in the framework of the nation state. It refers to the willingness to recognize people we do not know as part of the same political community. (Habermas repeatedly speaks of "solidarity among unknown people, strangers – "unter Fremden");

9 See Peters, Bernhard, "Deliberative Demokratie", in Wingert, Lutz, Günther, Klaus (Hg.), *Die Öffentlichkeit der Vernunft und die Vernunft der Öffentlichkeit*, Frankfurt/Main, Suhrkamp, 2001.

- in fact we should not confuse cultural identity, the sense of belonging to specific traditions (religious, linguistic…) or places or landscapes, with political identity; nor the identity of the individual with the identity of the citizen;
- and we should not mistake Europe for the European Union. Europe exists and will keep on existing, despite economic crises – unless there is a new continental drift –, and so exists a European culture, or more accurately European cultures, which everyone is free to define according to their own criteria – it is exactly the same at the national level; so the question is: how can we develop and anchor in these cultures a political identity and political habits – or to put another way: how can we, out of a *territory*, make a *space* of freedom, security and justice?[10]

The Issue of Sovereignty

The transnationalization of citizenship and the attempt to establish a democracy beyond national borders oblige us to rethink the concept of sovereignty, one of the two pillars of democracy along with individual rights. Here again we must admit that Europeans are tributary of different traditions. What is striking when reviewing this topic over the centuries is that, although sovereignty is usually characterized as perpetual, sacred, inviolable, the definition of sovereignty inevitably varies according to the historical circumstances.

If we look at the modern conceptions of sovereignty, from Jean Bodin, Thomas Hobbes, Jean-Jacques Rousseau, the American federalists, Benjamin Constant or Alexis de Tocqueville, it appears that each theory depends on a very particular historical context and tries to justify or to adapt to a new social or political situation, to a particular state of affairs. Each theory claims to provide a normative understanding of current events – but serves at the same time particular political interests. So that sovereignty is differently interpreted depending on the needs of the moment. We should keep this historical relativism in mind when we try to define what sovereignty should look like in a global age.

Let us sketch quickly the main characteristics of these theories.[11]

Jean Bodin in France in the 16th century (1530-1596) and Thomas Hobbes in England in the 17th (1588-1679) founded the modern political

---

10 Ferry, J.-M., *La république crépusculaire*, *op. cit.*, p. 77.

11 See Ferry, J.-M., "Les avatars de la souveraineté", in *La république crépusculaire*, *op. cit.*, pp. 161-234.

theory of absolute monarchy, along with a theory of absolute sovereignty. Both of them wrote in times of political and religious turmoil.

Jean Bodin wrote his main work *Les Six Livres de la République* in the context of the civil war between Protestants and Catholics in France. It was published in 1576, four years after the notorious St-Bartholomew's Day massacre. In his work, Bodin asserts the independence of political authorities from the Church, institutions like the Senate and the people. He considers the State not so much a power exercising control over a territory or a population by force or constraints – one of two main traditions of interpretation of a state's role – but as a legislating power. In so doing, he initiates the second tradition. He makes a distinction between the State, the Republic on the one hand and the government, the monarch on the other. Sovereignty is "the absolute and perpetual power of a Republic" (*Livre I, chap. VIII*). The monarch, incarnating this sovereignty, therefore possesses an absolute, indivisible and perpetual right to govern and to legislate. The purpose of politics, according to Bodin, is to reach cohesion between the Republic and a unified people under a unique, indivisible and perpetual authority. However, due to this distinction between State and Monarch, Republic and Sovereign, sovereignty contains its own *principles of self-limitation* because the Monarch is accountable to God and/or to the laws of nature. His actions must be in accordance with God or the cosmos, otherwise he would be a simple tyrant. The idea of *legitimacy* is therefore present in Bodin's reflections.

As is well known, Thomas Hobbes (1588-1679) wrote, like Bodin, in a context of religious and civil war. His purpose was to save the state from anarchy in a time of confrontations between Catholics and Protestants, between spiritual and temporal powers, and between Crown and Parliament. Like Bodin he thus justifies monarchic absolutism, but three essential features distinguish his theory from Bodin's: the idea of representation, the idea of a social contract, the absence of any religious or transcendent reference – let us say his functionalist and rationalist understanding of politics. The people are sovereign, not the monarch, but, according to Hobbes' theory of representation, they do not exercise power. The people are unified and personified in the State, perceived as a great person, the "Leviathan". The sovereign and the represented merge into a unique person. This fusion allows the people to identify with the monarch. Hobbes' theory is useful because it contains both pre-democratic and pre-liberal features: pre-democratic insofar as sovereignty is not anchored in a divine transcendence but in the *consent* of the people; pre-liberal insofar as the contract implies fundamental rights that must be preserved.

However precursory this theory may be, it draws, like Bodin's, on the Christian and medieval theory of the person and on the theologico-political medieval imagination. The image of the body of the sovereign (Prince or Leviathan) is central and reminds us of the medieval "christomimesis", that is the personification of God by the Emperor; the attributes of sovereignty (such as perpetual, indivisible, absolute) refer to the Christian theory of the person, developed for instance by Thomas Aquinas, and conceived of as "self-consistent, indivisible and incommunicable".[12]

Jean-Jacques Rousseau (1712-1778), another great theoretician of sovereignty, also defends absolutism, but this time *democratic* absolutism. Like Hobbes, he wonders how the masses can become a people. But, as we know, he rejects the idea of representation. "Power can be passed on", he argues, "but not will" ("Le pouvoir peut bien se transmettre, mais non pas la volonté").[13] The people are sovereign; they represent the source and the exercise of this sovereignty. No division and no duality are permitted. To solve the problem of cohesion, of the unity and autonomy of the political body, Rousseau invents the concept of "general will": the sovereignty of the people expresses itself through the general will. For Hobbes, the social contract was a way to establish sovereignty; for Rousseau, the contract is the purpose of political union. This concept of general will is a *moral concept*. Unlike Hobbes who focuses on instrumental rationality, Rousseau highlights the morality of the people. His theory of the general will is probably the best attempt to *merge the moral community and the legal community* and to define democracy by popular will. But only at the price of very strong idealism. Indeed, Rousseau confessed himself, as we know, that there could not be any real democracy on earth: only a people of gods could form a democracy ("S'il y avait un peuple de dieux, il se gouvernerait démocratiquement. Un gouvernement si parfait ne convient pas à des hommes").[14]

Bodin, Hobbes and Rousseau advocate, each in his own way, *absolute sovereignty*.

With Benjamin Constant, Tocqueville and the American federalists a new conception of sovereignty, a *liberal* one, develops at the turn of the 19th century. Constant and Tocqueville, in the context of the French Restoration, stand for a *limited sovereignty*, whereas Publius (1787-1789), the name under which James Madison (1751-1836), Alexander Hamilton (1757-1804) and John Jay (1745-1829) published the *Federalist Papers*, in the very particular context of the foundation of the United States of America, advocates the conception of a *shared or divided sovereignty*.

---

12 *Ibid.*, p. 169.

13 Rousseau, Jean-Jacques, *Du contrat social*, Livre II, Chapitre I, Paris, GF-Flammarion, 1992, p. 51.

14 Rousseau, J.-J., *Du contrat social*, Livre III, Chapitre IV, p. 97.

For Benjamin Constant (1767-1830), the key question is not: *who* is in power but how much power is at stake and how much power is exercised? He therefore introduces two principles which form the two pillars of a modern constitutional state:

- a democratic one: he recognizes that the source of sovereignty is the people;
- and a liberal one: the general will must exercise only limited authority over individuals.

Though he compares the political and collective freedom of the Ancient and the individual freedom of the Modern, he clearly believes in the superior legitimacy of the latter and expects the State to protect these individual rights. "May the state take care of justice", he says, "we will look after our happiness" ("Que l'Etat se borne à être juste, nous nous chargerons d'être heureux").[15] His anti-contractualist approach is based on a strong intuition: *individualism* is the main anthropological feature of the coming century.

The American Federalists, Madison, Hamilton and Jay, published during the period 1787-9 their reflections on the Union, the Constitution and sovereignty in the so called *Federalist Papers*. Their major concern, like many political thinkers of their time, was to avoid both despotism (of a universal monarchy or of the majority in a democracy) and anarchism (of a democracy). They were inspired by Montesquieu's idea of a federative Republic and defended the idea of a republican federation guaranteed by a Constitution for their country. (Cf. *Esprit des Lois*, Livre IX, chap. I.) They questioned whether sovereignty could be shared without being divided and weakened.

The idea of shared sovereignty suggests that each member state virtually holds a part of this sovereignty, while sovereignty can be properly actualized only with the union of all the States making up the Confederation.[16] In fact, as became obvious during the Secession War if not earlier, the American constitution recognizes no right to secede. This shows that, in the end, the Union prevails over the member states. That is one reason among others to state that the legal structure of European Union cannot be compared with the legal structure of the United States of America. In Europe, the member states have the right to secede. The truth is that national sovereignty remains particularly strong here.

[15] Constant, Benjamin, *De la liberté des Anciens comparée à celle des Modernes* (1819), in Colas, D., *La Pensée Politique*, Paris, Larousse, 1992, p. 429.

[16] Ferry, J.-M., *La république crépusculaire*, *op. cit.*, p. 229.

Based on this very quick review of a few famous theories of sovereignty we can draw the following conclusions:

- Theories depend on time and space. We can find no unique homogeneous concept of sovereignty. It may be absolute, limited, shared, and today, for instance for Habermas and deliberative democracy theorists, *procedural*, dissolved in deliberation and decision-making procedures.
- A philosopher like Gérard Mairet, a great connoisseur of the type of sovereignty put forward by Bodin and Hobbes, goes so far as to say that real democracy must be thought outside the conceptual framework of sovereignty because real sovereignty, with its attributes of unicity and submission to one body, or to one absolute representative, is in essence monarchic. And Rousseau only demonstrated that democratic absolutism is a contradiction in itself (he confessed that there could not be any real democracy on earth: only a people of gods could form a democracy). We could even question the notion of the general will, not only that of Rousseau, but more generally, and ask what kind of metaphysical representations are involved here; perhaps we should accept that the people as a whole *do not want.*[17]
- According to G. Mairet, sovereignty is in fact tied up with the construction of a state, and democracy tends to dissolve sovereignty and its homogenizing driving force. In this respect, democracy is by nature transnational or cosmopolitan.[18]
- Nevertheless, the truth is that nation states have so far managed to match state sovereignty and popular sovereignty, as if they were two faces of the same coin. But we should not mix them up and so deduce that the end of absolute state sovereignty hails the decline of popular sovereignty. Because, on the one hand, it is unclear whether state sovereignty is weakening inasmuch as cooperation and interdependence increase the capacity to solve global issues (in matters of peace, security, economy, environment…); loss of autonomy for a single state does not mean loss of sovereignty (if we understand state *sovereignty as the ability to solve political problems*, and not as absolute autonomy and independence);[19] on the other hand, even if we claim a decline in state sovereignty, by dissociating, conceptually, state sovereignty and popular sovereignty, we can

17 The wordplay is difficult to translate from French into English: volonté générale / le peuple ne veut pas.

18 Ferry, J.-M., *La république crépusculaire*, *op. cit.*, p. 239.

19 See Beck, Ulrich, *Power in the Global Age*, Cambridge (MA), Polity Press, 2006.

> save popular sovereignty from such decline. And after all, perhaps we should not be so nostalgic of the time when state sovereignty and popular sovereignty belonged together, so to say, because it was also the time when popular sovereignty was paid for at the very high price of the possible sacrifice of citizens for their nation.

Perhaps we can interpret the progressive dissociation of state sovereignty from popular sovereignty as civilizational progress and as a way of distancing oneself from an understanding of politics as decisionism. The EU seems to have chosen the new way out of decisionism and confrontation between friends and enemies, by using the "gentle civilizer",[20] to quote Martti Koskenniemi, that is, the rule of law, and the exchange of goods and arguments. This undoubtedly implies, for the member states, limited state sovereignty and shared popular sovereignty.

Jürgen Habermas has been dealing with this complex of problems for several years now. I believe that his interpretation of sovereignty is perhaps more operational and promising than others in a context of globalization and transnationalization of social and political issues.

Habermas *historicizes* the concept of sovereignty and shows how state sovereignty and popular sovereignty once overlapped. If we understand democracy as self-determination, Habermas confesses, it is true that the state used to help the people in implementing their capacity to act collectively. Popular sovereignty once relied on state sovereignty to express itself. And, if necessary, the sovereign state went to war to defend the integrity of popular sovereignty beyond national borders.[21] But, Habermas argues, they are not conceptually tied up with each other. In a context of complex interconnections like ours, the people's capacity to act must be played out, most of time, on a transnational or supranational level. Even the strongest nation states have to cooperate in matters of energy, transport, communication, environment, economy… and accept a relativization and a reduction of their national sovereignty.

Popular sovereignty is not so much regarded by Habermas as a legislative power, but rather as a contesting force, as a communicative power, expressing the needs and expectations of a very diverse civil society and trying to influence decision makers at different levels in the public sphere: informal, media and political public sphere. That is why Habermas speaks about a "dissolved sovereignty". He has waved goodbye to the fantasy

20 Koskenniemi, Martti, *The Gentle Civilizer of Nations: The Rise and Fall of International Law 1870-1960*, Cambridge, Cambridge University Press, 2001.

21 See e.g. Habermas, J., "Ein Ruck muss durch Europa gehen", in *Die Weltwoche*, No. 21, 19 mai 2004.

of a united nation represented by a unique body. Communicative power circulates through many different channels.

In his review of Kant's *Treaty of perpetual peace*,[22] Habermas suggests that Kant could have developed further the idea of a league of nation states, if he had had in mind not the French Revolution and the French Republican state that established strict reciprocity between state and popular sovereignties, but the American Revolution and the federalist model that relied on the idea of shared sovereignty between local, national and federal levels. In other words, the constitutionalization of international relationships (at a European or even a global level) is possible if we understand that constitution and state, in the liberal tradition, to which Habermas refers, are not conceptually linked. Whereas the Rousseauist conception of social contract institutes in the same founding gesture a constitution, a State and a people of citizens, the liberal tradition considers that the constitution has no authority to institute sovereignty, but only to limit the excesses of the power (herrschaftsgründend vs. machtbegrenzend). What founds here the rule of law (Rechtsstaat) is, more than the unity of a popular will and a constitution, the separation of powers. In this tradition, the rule of law imposes limits on politics and restrains power.

In fact, Habermas demonstrates the co-originarity of republican and liberal points of view in *Between Facts and Norms*,[23] thus allowing him to escape the never-ending opposition between republican and liberal traditions. Habermas does not want to favour the liberal at the expense of the republican tradition: he wants to show that *the best normative understanding* of present times tends to consider them as *co-originary*.

The Transnational Order

Habermas says that a transnational democratic order is conceivable and possible provided we unlock certain "mental locks".[24] The question of identity and the question of sovereignty are two important locks. But springing these locks does not imply that we have to get rid of the nation state.

Jean-Marc Ferry suggests conceiving of transnational democracy as organized on three levels. He argues that the dynamic of the European integration should not be understood as a shift from international law to cosmopolitan law, but as the coexistence of three levels: internal,

---

22 Habermas, J., "Kants Idee des ewigen Friedens – aus dem historischen Abstand von 200 Jahren", in *Die Einbeziehung des Anderen*, Frankfurt/Main, Suhrkamp, 1996.

23 Habermas, J., *Between Facts and Norms*, Cambridge (MA), MIT Press, 1998.

24 Habermas, J., *Zur Verfassung Europas*, *op. cit.*

international – more precisely the law of peoples ("droit des gens") – and cosmopolitan law.[25]

- The first level is the national level: internal law organizes the legal relationships between fellow citizens and provides fundamental rights (civil, political, social, cultural rights). The national level remains essential as it is here that democratic legitimacy is formed, relevant topics are triggered, political participation takes place, and citizenship is concretely experienced and exercised.
- The second level is the law of peoples: the law of peoples refers to the relationships between nation states, but also between or towards peoples that do not form a state, perhaps forming a minority within a state in Europe. As already noted in the first section of this paper, the originality of the EU, according to Ferry, is that this second level is more developed in its legal structure than in general international law. Values of integrity, participation, solidarity and personality that were so far only attached to individual fundamental rights are transposed to the level of relationships between peoples:
  - integrity: this refers to the principles of territorial integrity and self-determination of peoples (it is not a specificity of the EU);
  - participation: negatively, member-states have a right to secede from the EU; positively, they participate in the elaboration of common policy, according to the principles of co-sovereignty and co-responsibility;
  - solidarity: this refers to the existing mechanisms of redistribution, of equalization between the different member-states and regions of the EU;
  - personality: the EU recognizes the cultural rights of nations and of the peoples of Europe, even minorities like gypsies and travellers, recognizing their collective identities, languages, cultures, memories, histories.
- The third level is the level of cosmopolitan law. It is just starting to be implemented. It refers to the growing role of the European Court of Justice. It also refers to the free movement right and the right to install oneself in a European country irrespective of one's nationality, and it refers also to civic rights: the rights to vote at the European Parliament and to vote at local elections. The truth is that only few European citizens make concrete use of this European citizenship: one estimate suggests that only 5% of the European

[25] Ferry, J.-M., *La république crépusculaire*, *op. cit.*, pp. 123-124.

population actively exercise European citizenship.[26] It is no wonder then that most people do not feel like European citizens. They are simply unaware that they are holders of this citizenship which can be renewed anytime.

This three-level structure may offer *the normative framework* of the EU – and prevent us from conceiving the EU in national patterns, as if its similarity with the nation state were the criterion of its success or failure. However, in order to increase the democratic legitimacy inside this three-level structure and to make sure that popular sovereignty does not get lost in this transnational organization, reforms have to be implemented.

- The EU should distance itself from the strong "inter-governmentalism" and "executive federalism" trends that have so far prevailed.[27] This executive federalism, symbolized by the dominant role of the European Council and the Franco-German partnership, is partly responsible for the lack of democratic legitimacy in the European Union.
- According to Habermas, the Lisbon Treaty seems headed in the right direction:[28]

Let us mention a few reforms:[29]

The powers of the European Parliament are extended:

- in the legislative domain: with the extension of the legislative co-decision procedure (shared by the Council of Ministers and the Parliament), extension to nearly 50 new areas.
- in the budgetary area: The European Parliament has been given a right to decision equal to that of the Council of Ministers, notably with regard to the adoption of the entire annual budget.
- In terms of political control: The Parliament elects the President of the Commission (position occupied by José Manuel Barroso) on the proposal of the European Council. Parliament has to take into account the results of the European elections, along with the majority that won. This should lead to a politicization of the European elections.

In addition, the Lisbon Treaty sets out the role to be played by national parliaments. They check that competences are being shared between the

---

[26] See Cheneval, Francis, contribution to Chopin, T., Lacroix, J. (ed.), "Démocratie: la voie européenne", in www.raison-publique.fr, 09 March 2010.

[27] Habermas, J., *Zur Verfassung Europas*, *op. cit.*

[28] See article by V. Beširević in the present volume.

[29] See Robert Schuman Foundation: www.robert.schuman.eu.

Union and the Member States thanks to the introduction of an "early-warning mechanism". This mechanism must allow each national parliament to indicate when the subsidiarity principle is in danger of being violated by the European institutions.

Let us also mention:

- the fact that the Council of Ministers have to meet in public (which was not previously the case) when a "law" is debated and approved. Journalists can therefore inform citizens about debates that are taking place within the Council.
- A new rule of double majority was introduced for the decisions taken by the Council: it takes into account the weight of populations and hence is more democratic.

A last remark concerning democracy and sovereignty within the EU. The question is frequently asked: who is the "pouvoir constituant" in the EU? The three-level structure suggests that there are two "sujets constituants", two sources of sovereignty: the citizens of the EU and the member-states. In his book *Zur Verfassung Europas*, Habermas identifies these two coexisting sources of sovereignty, but goes a little further and explains that we should see behind the member-states, the people, national citizens a as source of sovereignty, so that each citizen is somehow *a double holder of sovereignty*, as a European citizen, represented directly at the supranational level in the European Parliament, and as a national citizen, represented indirectly by his or her government in the Council. From this perspective, sovereignty is shared between the two roles played by each citizen, and transnationalizing sovereignty should not decrease democratic legitimacy. But of course reforms should be continued until these two "sujets constituants" are equal partners and equal right holders in all legislative matters.

One concluding remark: perhaps we should not expect too much from the EU, at least no messianism, no super State, no classical constitution with 20 easy-to-read articles – as Thomas Paine demanded. Indeed, we may consider this good news because it means that we have already almost everything we need within our nation states (which seems to prove Kant right, as we said in our introduction, when he explained that people do not want to give up their national specificities). The EU should therefore be understood as a political and legal structure *sui generis* that helps us to preserve our democratic ways of life in a context of globalization and global challenges – and that also provides us, positively, a few new possibilities of living.

On European Multiculturalism

Patrice Canivez

The starting point of this analysis is Charles Taylor's distinction between multiculturalism and interculturalism. The distinction refers to the Canadian context; it reflects the contrast between Anglophone and Francophone Canada. In an article published in *Philosophy and Social Criticism*,[1] however, Taylor clarifies the concept of interculturalism and gives it a wider scope, explaining why this concept applies to European countries. I will first discuss this theory (I), pointing out that if the concept of interculturalism is suitable for each or most European countries, it does not apply to the European Union (EU) as such. Considered as a whole, the EU is a multicultural entity. I will then inquire into the specificity of European multiculturalism (II). Such multiculturalism is closely related to the political structure of the EU, which leads me to discuss Habermas' understanding of Europe's constitutional problems (III). It seems that there is a shift in Habermas' position on this matter, witness his current insistence on the concept of transnational democracy (in *Zur Verfassung Europas*),[2] as opposed to that of a postnational polity (in his writings on the *postnationale Konstellation*).[3] Finally, I shall suggest that Habermas' position would benefit from the use of the concept of interculturalism as defined by Taylor.

I. Multiculturalism vs. Interculturalism (Charles Taylor)

Charles Taylor rejects the opposition that is usually made between multiculturalism and socio-political integration. On the one hand, he criticizes the idea that multiculturalism encourages people, especially

---

1 See Taylor, Ch., "Interculturalism or Multiculturalism?", in *Philosophy and Social Criticism*, 2012, 38 (4-5), pp. 413-423.

2 Habermas, J., *Zur Verfassung Europas. Ein Essay*, Berlin, Suhrkamp Verlag, 2011. English version by Ciaran Cronin, *The Crisis of the European Union: A Response*, Cambridge (UK)/Malden (MA, USA), 2012.

3 Habermas, J., *Die postnationale Konstellation. Politische Essays*, Frankfurt am Main, Suhrkamp Verlag, 1998. English Version by Max Pensky, *The Postnational Constellation. Political Essays*, Cambridge, Massachusetts, The MIT Press, 2001.

immigrants, to retreat into closed cultural communities and thus leads to ghettoization. In his view, the vast majority of immigrants are willing to integrate into the host society. Ghettoization does not result from too much recognition of cultural differences, but from a mix of discrimination and lack of opportunities:

> The major motivation of immigrants into rich democracies is to find new opportunities, of work, education, or self-expression, for themselves and especially for their children. If they manage to secure these, they – and even more their children – are happy to integrate into the society. It is only if this hope is frustrated, if the path to more rewarding work and education is blocked, that a sense of alienation and hostility to the receiving society can grow, and may even generate a rejection of the mainstream and its ethic.[4]

Thus, when correctly understood, the purpose of multiculturalism is not only the recognition of differences; it is also the achievement of more social integration and equality. In other words, multiculturalism is closely linked to the development of liberal and democratic principles. However, the term "multiculturalism" may be understood in a larger or a more restricted sense. In the wider sense, the word refers to a policy that aims at: a) recognizing cultural differences, and b) facilitating the social and political integration of immigrants. Multiculturalism in the narrow sense of the word is a way of achieving those aims, while interculturalism is another. In fact, what distinguishes multi- and interculturalism is not so much the policies that are pursued. In practical terms, multiculturalism and interculturalism lead to very similar policies. In Canada, for instance, they justify the practice of "reasonable accommodation", notably in public schools and offices. Therefore, the main difference between the two concepts lies in the "stories" they tell or to which they refer. It lies in the "rhetoric" that puts integration in a certain perspective. One could say that multiculturalism gives greater weight to the recognition of pluralism while interculturalism puts the stress on integration. Behind this apparently merely rhetorical difference, however, there is the contrast between Quebec and the rest of Canada. In Anglophone Canada, the majority of the population has long been of British descent – meaning English, Scottish, and Irish. Consequently, there was a correspondence between the dominant culture and the social composition of the citizenry. In Taylor's terms, there was a strong "anglo-normativity". However, this is no longer the case. Anglophone Canada is now made up of a plurality of communities among which people of British descent are a minority – approximately a third of the population, according to Taylor. Another factor is the social advance of citizens of non-British origin who have made

4 Taylor, Ch., art. cit., p. 414.

their way to positions of importance in all walks of life. Consequently, the "anglo-normative identity" is not dominant anymore – or tends to lose its predominance. Of course, this is an English-speaking society, but the English language is a mere vehicle for social integration and political participation. In Quebec, the situation is quite different. Up to 70 per cent of the Quebeckers are from French descent. And as everybody knows, the policy of Quebec is to preserve a francophone culture that defines the historical identity of the Quebeckers.

This sociological and historical background accounts for the distinction between multi- and interculturalism. In Taylor's view, multiculturalism and interculturalism are two different patterns of cultural relationships. As we have seen, both multiculturalism and interculturalism are ways of accommodating cultural pluralism and facilitating integration. In the case of multiculturalism, however, integration means integration into society. Immigrants must find jobs, develop their life projects, perform their civic duties, etc. The use of a common language – i.e. English – is culturally neutral. It enables people from different backgrounds and communities to interact with each other. In the case of interculturalism, integration does not only mean integration into society. It means integration into a specific culture. Immigrants are not only supposed to play their part in the development of society. They are also supposed to play their part in the preservation and development of the host culture, that is, of the francophone culture. Here lies the main difference between the "stories" that are told by the two concepts:

> The 'multi' story decentres the traditional ethno-historical identity and refuses to put any other in its place. All such identities coexist in the society, but none is officialized. The 'inter' story starts from the reigning historical identity but sees it evolving in a process in which all citizens, of whatever identity, have a voice, and no-one's input has a privileged status.[5]

Taylor's distinction between multi- and interculturalism is at the same time interesting and questionable. Every language carries its own historical heritage. By this I do not mean that any language is in itself the bearer of ethical values, which is obviously not true. I mean that a historical heritage is more or less embedded in the social and cultural institutions – schools, universities, academic curricula, etc. – in which the language is taught and practised. Learning the language in attending these schools and universities, reading the books that make up the classical curriculum, entail a process of acculturation that is not neutral. However, what I am interested in is the fact that Taylor, at the end of the paper he published in *Philosophy and Social Criticism*, states that the Quebecker notion of interculturalism might serve as a model for European nation-states. For

[5] *Ibid.*, p. 418.

in the European nation-states, there is a national culture that is the culture of the majority of the population, if not of all. Integration into the host country means integration into the national culture of the country. At the same time, such integration of newcomers is a key factor in the development of the national culture. It encourages the host culture to enlarge its perspectives and open up to new interpretations.

II. Multiculturalism in Europe

The distinction between multiculturalism and interculturalism refers to the Canadian context. However, the concept of interculturalism applies also to the European nations, at least to most of them. As Taylor puts it:

> The features which make it applicable to Quebec also often apply in Europe. There: (1) many countries have a long-standing historic identity which is still shared by the great majority of their citizens; (2) this identity frequently centres around a language which is not spoken elsewhere, and is under pressure from larger, 'globalized' languages; and (3) the same kind of not-fully-structured fears for the future of its culture and way of life may arise there as I noted in Quebec. Points (1) and (2) make the intercultural story a better fit than the multicultural one.[6]

Thus, in Europe as in Quebec, interculturalism could be a way of integrating minorities and newcomers in enabling them to take part in the development of the host society and culture. This supposes that immigrants and/or minority members be treated as equals, that is, as partners in such a development. However, here lies a problem. In most European societies, there is a fear that newcomers might alter the majority culture and way of life, a fear that "they" might change "us". Or in a more negative way, there is a fear that immigrants do not even want to transform the host culture, but to create their own self-contained communities within the host society. Hence, the demand that immigrants and minority members adopt the same customs and way of life as "old-stock" nationals. Learning the national language and adopting the same basic ethic are not enough. Immigrants should be "like us". Assimilation becomes the condition of integration, while policies advocating strict limitation of immigration and the return of immigrants to their countries become popular. Inasmuch as such fears and distrust generate marginalization and make it more difficult for immigrants to access jobs, housing, etc., the result is precisely what should be prevented, that is, a tendency to ghettoization and a resentment towards the host society that, in its turn, fuels the fears and suspicion of the majority. Thus, a sort of vicious circle sets

6 *Ibid.*, p. 420.

in, which in Taylor's view should and could be reversed. In order to do that, it is necessary to reach out to leaders of the minorities and newcomers, consider them as partners and co-deciders, in a word: implement the intercultural scenario. If successful, the enactment of this scenario can generate a sense of gratitude and a form of patriotism – as may be seen in the USA – among immigrants whose main desire is to integrate into the host society in order to have a better life for themselves and their children.

Taylor's conception of social integration may seem exaggeratedly optimistic, but it is not. Interculturalism is necessary to overcome fears and mutual distrust. At the same time, however, putting aside such fears and distrust is necessary to bring about interculturalism and make it work. Here again, there is a circle that can either end up in a deadlock, or evolve into a positive process, the overcoming of distrust making interculturalism possible, the successful implementation of interculturalism making it then easier to further reduce mutual distrust. In the following, I will not discuss the chances of such a virtuous circle, which depends on the specific context and the mode of governance of each country. What I am interested in, is the general idea that multiculturalism presupposes a set of common standards that are more or less neutral inasmuch as they do not reflect the predominance of a majority culture, while interculturalism refers to the inner enlargement of a national culture that benefits from the participation, new ideas and interpretations provided by minorities and newcomers – a process, it is worth noting, which already takes place through the succession of generations, each one reinterpreting in its own way the common culture.

Taylor is right in saying that such a way of accommodating pluralism is best suited to most European countries. However, it does not apply to the European Union (EU) as such. In contrast to its member states, the EU is an instance of multiculturalism rather than of interculturalism. This is obvious as regards the use of a common language. The use of English as a common language is neutral in the sense that it is not the language of a dominant nation. We could even experience a very peculiar situation. If the United Kingdom were to opt out of the European Union in the referendum of 2017, the Europeans' common language would be a foreign tongue for all of them, except the Irish. However, if we want to go deeper into the question, we have to take a closer look at the overall situation. From a purely descriptive point of view, the cultural diversity of Europe is huge. There are 28 member states and roughly 500 million inhabitants in the EU. There are 24 official languages and many more if we take dialects and regional languages into account. The diversity is also religious. Europe is one of the "meeting points" of the "religions of the Book": Catholicism, Islam, Judaism, Orthodoxy and the diverse denominations of Protestantism. Paradoxically, the most striking traits of the EU are often overlooked. When we think of the EU, for instance, we are mostly focused on the so-called big countries: Germany, France, the United Kingdom and, to a lesser extent, Italy, Poland and Spain. It is true that if we add up the population of these six countries, it amounts to more than two-thirds of the European population. However, when considering the European member states, the vast majority of them are small countries. Three quarters of the EU member states have less than 20 million inhabitants. When – and if – the EU becomes politically mature, the question is whether it is going to be a political organisation where a vast majority of small states is led by a minority of larger ones or if this political asymmetry will be offset by different kinds of political alliances between the smaller ones. Apart from the difference in size and population, however, we must take into account the political idiosyncrasies of the EU member states. Of course, they are all supposed to be democratic states, although some of them are dangerously drifting away, like Viktor Orbán's Hungary. But there are huge differences that are inherited from the past. The most obvious difference is that between republics and monarchies. The important symbolic role of historic monarchies in some EU member states suffices to indicate how difficult it is to conceive of a politically integrated European Union. Moreover, there are different types of nation-states in Europe. In Central Europe, the typical nation-state consists of a nation coexisting with its minorities – for instance, the Hungarian minority in Rumania. In Western Europe, such a pattern does not apply. Neither the Scots in the UK nor the Turks in Germany are minorities in the sense the Hungarians are in Rumania. There are also significant differences in the patterns of political integration. There are centralized states like France, federal states like Germany, consociations like Belgium, etc. All these states have distinctive narrative identities. They have a strong sense of their historic identity.

Now, when dealing with the question of a European multiculturalism, we must determine in what sense we speak of multiculturalism. In fact, the word "multiculturalism" applies to the European context in two, maybe three different ways. First, the word refers to the diverse national cultures. Europe is a multicultural society in the sense of a plurality of cultures that coexist on the basis of a common set of values and modes of communication. Second, the word refers to the way each EU member state accommodates its own internal pluralism. Third, there is a sort of multiculturalism that results from the European "endomigration" or internal migration. By that I mean people migrating from one European country to another: Poles settling in the UK, Spaniards migrating to Germany, the particular case of the Roma, etc. This is nothing new: the history of Europe is not only a history of religious, linguistic and political conflicts. It is also a history of constant migrations of people and ideas across the continent.

These three kinds of multiculturalism raise different types of issues. For instance, the way each nation-state accommodates its own cultural pluralism depends on the origin of this pluralism. Some nation-states are constitutively multinational. Some others are multicultural because of a constant flux of immigrants. As Will Kymlicka has shown, the difference between multinational and polyethnic societies[7] calls for different kinds of solutions. A multinational society is not multicultural in the same way a society of immigrants is. Another type of question is raised by the theologico-political factor. When it comes to multiculturalism, two issues are particularly sensitive: the linguistic and the religious issues. Nowadays, the question of multiculturalism is in large part the question of Islam. It is due to the presence of an important Muslim population in the major European countries. The attitude towards Islam, however, depends on the relationships between the religious and the political in each country. The process of secularization has developed in different ways in each of the EU member states. The type of relationship between church and state that prevails in each of them determines their perception of the multicultural issue. Hence the question is: can we conceive of a convergence between the EU member policies as regards the accommodation of religious and linguistic minorities? There must be some kind of unification in the way European states deal with their inner cultural diversity. This requires, for instance, a joint policy with respect to immigration, the rights of minorities, etc.

Finally, the multinational nature of the EU itself is a specific issue. Here, the question arises: is the goal of the EU to preserve the different national cultures, to ensure not only their preservation but also the conditions to enable them to develop? Or, to put it in a more caustic way, must we conceive of the EU as a museum of national cultures? In order to answer the question, we must take up the issue of EU political integration. That is why I would like to make a few comments on Habermas' concept of a European transnational democracy. Habermas' theories on Europe have been intensively discussed. In the following, however, I will focus on the shift from the "postnational" to the "transnational" because such a shift has a bearing on the issue of multiculturalism.

III. Postnational vs. Transnational Democracy (Jürgen Habermas)

Habermas has developed his views on Europe in many texts, articles and conferences over the past twenty years or so. His main views are constant. First, in a globalized world, socio-economic processes cannot be

[7] See Kymlicka, W., *Multicultural Citizenship*, Oxford, Clarendon Press, 1995.

politically controlled and regulated at the level of the nation-state. Such political control requires that the nation-states come together and achieve some sort of supra-national polity. Second, with respect to the European project, this means that the goal of the European Union is not only to secure peace among the European nations. The goal of the Union is, or should be, to make common action possible. Peaceful coexistence is a tremendous achievement of the European Union. What we need now is an EU that enables us to engage in joint political action. Third, the aim of the EU should not be – or should not only be – to become a global player like China or the USA. The achievement of political integration at European level is a first step on the way to cosmopolitanism. Thus the political integration of Europe should serve as a model for the global governance that is needed in a globalized world.

These are Habermas' constant ideas. However, there has been a noticeable evolution in his conception of Europe. At the end of the 1990s, Habermas spoke of the "postnational constellation" and contemplated the prospect of a European Federation. In his view, there were "no structural obstacles to expanding national civic solidarity and welfare-state policies to the scale of a postnational federation",[8] even though it was obvious that "a constitution for a multinational state on the scale of the European Union cannot simply adopt the model of constitutions of national federations such as the Federal Republic of Germany".[9] More precisely, two questions had to be asked: first, "whether the European Union can [...] compensate for the lost competencies of the nation-state"; and second, "whether political communities form a collective identity beyond national borders, and thus whether they can meet the legitimacy conditions for a postnational democracy". Habermas insisted that "if these two last questions can't be answered affirmatively, then a Federal States of Europe is ruled out, and with it the basis for any broader hopes".[10] However, Habermas now speaks of a "transnational democracy" and insists that Europe is neither a Federal state nor a Federation of nations. The shift is noticeable when comparing Habermas' two major writings on the question: *Die postnationale Konstellation*, which dates back to 1998, and *Zur Verfassung Europas*, which was published in 2011.

Let's examine the use Habermas made of the concept of multiculturalism in the *Postnational Constellation*. Apart from the fact that the nation-state is no match for world markets, he insisted on the growing multiculturalism in the major European nation-states. This he saw as a

8 Habermas, J., *The Postnational Constellation*, *op. cit.*, p. 108.

9 *Ibid.*, p. 99.

10 *Ibid.*, p. 90.

fact but also as an opportunity. His line of argument was the following. In the 19th and 20th century, the nation-state was the right framework for political action. The national sentiment could be a source of aggressive nationalism, but it was also a sentiment of solidarity among citizens. It enabled citizens to accept solidarity measures between the richer and the poorer. It supported the development of a social security network, of a redistribution of resources, etc. However, the development of national feelings supposed a certain level of cultural homogeneity among citizens. And the point is that such cultural homogeneity is no longer possible. All modern nation-states are more and more internally diversified. Immigration, individualism and the unstoppable flow of information across the globe make for the increasing pluralism of all developed societies. In this respect, Habermas' view was that a shift from the national to the postnational was necessary to restore the possibility of effective political action. But his idea was also that such a change of paradigm was an opportunity to liberate the citizens' political participation from the constraints of nation-state politics and the closure of the ethno-national mindset. "Post-national" did not mean that nation-states were not to exist anymore. It was a kind of *Aufhebung* in the Hegelian sense of the word: nation-states were destined to integrate in a more effective and meaningful political organization.

In his most recent texts on Europe, however, Habermas speaks of a transnational democracy. In great part, the use of the word transnational means that the EU is not and should not become a super-state. The experience of the last decade, especially the collapse of the EU Constitutional project in 2005 and the Merkel-Sarkozy condominium, has led Habermas to fear that a supranational Europe would give rise to some sort of "post-democratic" federalism, which is an "executive federalism" (*Exekutivföderalismus*).[11] As against such post-democratic super-state, Habermas now advocates the development of a transnational democracy. In order to sustain his view, he invokes different reasons. From a constitutional point of view, for instance, there is a fundamental reason why the EU cannot be a Federal State. Roughly speaking, the reason is that the EU and the member states share the sovereignty. Between the EU and the member states, there is a complex relationship that has nothing to do with the inclusion of the German *Länder* in the *Bundesrepublik* or with the incorporation of the American states in the USA. It is true that European laws and directives prevail over national legislations, but only in the fields of competence that are explicitly attributed to the EU by the member states. Unlike all Federations, the EU has no competence over

[11] Habermas, J., *Zur Verfassung Europas*, *op. cit.*, p. 8.

its own competences. The member states are partners of the EU; they are not subordinated to it. As regards EU citizens, they remain the ultimate source of political legitimacy. However, they must consider themselves, at the same time, as citizens of the EU and as citizens of their nation-state. Eventually, one of the main reasons why the nation-states may not and should not be sublated, *aufgehoben* in a European Federal State, is that nation-states have succeeded in securing a certain level of political and social rights. In this respect, the idea of a postnational polity must be re-evaluated. Back in the 1990s, the postnational perspective appeared to be the right way to disconnect political participation from the closure of national identities and loyalties. Now, it seems to entail the risk of regressing below the level of political and social rights that has been achieved at nation-state level. Hence Habermas' revised position: after the shift from the national to the postnational, the shift from the postnational to the transnational.

In my opinion, there are also deeper reasons for such a move. Habermas' successive positions may be related to two of his fundamental critical attitudes: his anti-nationalism and his anti-state dispositions. On the one hand, he is apprehensive of the collusion between the political and the national. That is why he insisted, in the 1990s, that our present situation called for a disconnection between the political and the national. The development of new forms of political action and participation required that citizens liberate themselves from the constraints and limits of the national mindset. On the other hand, Habermas is defiant of the state. In his view, the very essence of the state is the institutionalization of power. His tradition of thought is that of Marx and Max Weber, it is not that of Aristotle, Rousseau and Hegel, which defines the state as a community of citizens. That is why Habermas repeatedly says, in his recent texts, that the state must be "civilized". There must be a "*Zivilisierung der staatlichen und gesellschaftlichen Gewaltverhältnisse*".[12] Such a *Zivilisierung* of the state is a remainder of Norbert Elias' *Prozeß der Zivilisation,*[13] which is a process of domestication and inhibition of violence. Applied to the state, the notion suggests that the state must be tamed and domesticated. In the republican tradition, however, the tradition that dates back to Plato and Aristotle and goes all the way down to Rousseau and Hegel, the state does not need to be civilized. What it needs is to be properly constituted. A state that is based on violence and arbitrary power is not a real state, but a sham of a state. In the republican tradition, the source of political legitimacy is the republican constitution. In Habermas' view, political

[12] *Ibid.*, p. 44. See also p. 57.

[13] Elias, N., *Über den Prozeß der Zivilisation*, Bern/München, Francke Verlag, 1969.

legitimacy comes from civil society. It is civil society, not the state that is the true *locus* of the political. The most significant part of political action – of communicative action – develops in the "horizontal dimension" of civil society, not through the "vertical relationship" between state and citizens. And when it comes to such "vertical relationship", the bottom-up influence of citizens on government administration is more significant than the top-down action of the administration.

If I am right, this accounts – at least, in part – for the evolution in Habermas' thinking. Ideally speaking, there should be a disconnection between the political and the national and, at the same time, between the state and the political. Political interaction and participation develop when people are neither fenced in by national identities nor impeached by state power. When it comes to the European political structure, however, things are complicated. When insisting on the necessity to free citizens from the closure of the national mind, Habermas stresses the virtue of a European post-national political community. When pointing out the threat of a post-democratic European super-state, he insists on the virtue of a "horizontal", transnational civil society. In the 1990s, the idea was to disconnect the political from the national. That was the idea of a European polity that opened the way to a European constitutional patriotism. Now he wants to disconnect the political from the state – meaning from the threat of a European post-democratic state – and in order to do so, he has to reconnect the political to the national.

But how is this conceivable if what used to be the nation's homogeneous culture no longer exists? In the 1990s, Habermas explained: a) that the sentiment of civic solidarity that made possible the redistribution of resources within the nation-state presupposed a homogeneous national culture, and b) that such homogeneity no longer existed. Now it seems that national cultures are more resilient and that we must count on the nation-states to maintain the cultural preconditions that are required in order to foster the sense of civic solidarity.

In fact, Charles Taylor's concept of interculturalism might be the solution. If we conceive of European nations as multicultural societies – meaning societies where the common political culture and social modes of communication do not reflect the prevalence of a given ethno-historic culture – the idea of a transnational democracy seems fragile. The notion of a *trans-national* democracy presupposes the existence of nations. On the part of citizens, it implies a sense of belonging to a given nation. Consequently, the notion of interculturalism is more consistent with the concept of transnational democracy, since interculturalism implies the existence of a majority, national culture, which is to be innerly enriched by newcomers. In a word, Habermas' transnational democracy needs

Taylor's interculturalism – at least, in the European context. National cultures are not being fragmented and deconstructed. They are undergoing a process of enlargement and reinterpretation as they integrate newcomers and new generations.

However, this is probably not the last word. For it remains that Habermas' concept of a transnational, non-federal democracy does not measure up to the problem he himself raises. If the goal of the EU is to set the conditions for a joint, effective political action of the member states, some kind of federal organization is needed. In fact, it already exists in many respects and it is building up, even if chaotically, in the Eurozone – witness the increasing role of the European Central Bank, the idea of a European Banking Union, which raise more and more insistently the problem of the political control of such federal institutions. In other words, the problem is to determine whether or not a federal administration needs a federal form of democratic control. If the answer is positive, such a federative polity does not have to be modelled on the pattern of already existing federations like the USA or the German Federation. It must be an original, specific kind of polity. In this view, Europeans should not walk away from the idea of federalism for fear that they might not be able to domesticate or civilize it. For federalism is already there in many respects. The problem is to give it a proper democratic constitution. Of course, there is no historic necessity, which means that Europeans may well be unable to solve the problem. The EU is a success as regards the achievement of peace, the level of prosperity, the guarantee of individual rights. At least it is enough of a success to remain attractive to current and potential candidate countries. But the EU might still prove to be a failure as regards the capacity to be a co-decider at world level. Within the coming world order, Europe might well turn out to be something like a postmodern variant of the *Heiliges Römisches Reich Deutscher Nation*. In the most favourable version of this scenario, the EU could evolve into a relatively secure, wealthy, culturally appealing and, politically, insignificant and irrelevant unit.

What Is Europe? Reflections on Derrida and Habermas

Tonči VALENTIĆ

Europe nowadays is facing a significant economic, political and social crisis. Although the idea of Europe has been widely discussed for centuries, today we are dealing with its urgent questioning: what is the aim of this project beyond all historical, cultural and political borders? The main idea of this article is to renew discussion of the idea of Europe in terms of its *philosophical* concepts. In the midst of a devastating economic crisis and a worrying political deficit, we must discuss the future of the European Union as a supra-national economic project, as well as the potential to form a new political identity and make a radical turn in order to renovate this project in the age of global post-democracy and media plutocracy. I argue that one of the main problems is that the ideal of Europe as a universal community, creating common cultural values, is still a utopian ideal. The main problem is the non-existence of Europe as a universal *political* community (i.e. a politically united peoples of Europe). In other words, Europe today is a post-imperial space at the end of history and involves peoples without power. There is an urgent need for structural change in the paradigm of social construction of reality. Contemporary global capitalism is based on techno-science, new media and a neoliberal economy; politics has become the domain of managerial elites and culture is reduced to celebrity culture; mass media events have become happenings without a message, turned into the visual semiotics of emptiness. To address these issues, I will focus on the works and ideas of two thinkers of Europe, who didn't always agree on these topics, but are nevertheless very important critics and indispensable thinkers of European project: Jacques Derrida and Jürgen Habermas.

Before further analysis, I will propose three main arguments: 1) The potential realization of the European project is basically a question of the possibility of action within the framework of liberal democracy, which is essentially the project of unfinished modernity.[1] The foundation of

[1] Noticeably, this is the outcome of controversies based upon Habermas' influential book *The Philosophical Discourse of Modernity*, Cambridge, Polity Press, 1987.

Europe is the Enlightenment's notion of freedom, reason and tolerance. Therefore, the question *What is Europe?* is not "one among other questions", as Derrida would say,[2] because at heart this question concerns the sustainability of ideas that determine the universality of the notion of the world. The future of "project Europe" is thus wrapped up in the global question about the meaning of politics in general. As far as Habermas is concerned, there will be no change in politics before building up institutional legal-political preconditions for different types of action. 2) We must separate the notion and idea of *Europe* from that of *European Union*. The above-mentioned crisis of Europe as a universal ideal is quite different from the economic crisis of European Union. The point is not simply to make a radical shift in political space, but also to change the politics of neoliberal capitalism. For in the case of the EU, neoliberal capitalism has taken on the role of the main generator of structural crisis, insofar as politicians in the EU have become managers and the EU does not serve the interests of European citizens and nation-states alike, but rather follows the brutal interests of transnational corporations. 3) There is a need to change "identity without power" to "power identity". I argue that one of the main advantages of the USA over Europe is that America is successful because it is the rule of *political power without cultural identity*, and in Europe we have *cultural identity without political power*.

These are the cornerstones of this essay. The main point is that Europe is not a geographically defined space inhabited with peoples who do or do not consider themselves Europeans, but is rather a universal *political* community, founded on spiritual values derived from the historical process of building Kantian "Perpetual Peace".[3] Let's first begin with Derrida's notion of Europe.

As Derrida wrote in the beginning of *The Other Headings: Reflections on Today's Europe*,[4] the question of Europe is not merely one question among others: it is a question that will always be of current interest. The question of Europe is "both a great opportunity and a danger", drawing its urgency and immediate relevance from the threat that we "no longer know very well *what* or *who* goes by this name". That said, for Derrida, Europe has always been in crisis. What is different today in Europe is that Europe may be about to realize the promise of its "concept", the very existence of which is "both a great opportunity and a danger". Taking up

---

2 See Derrida, Jacques, *The Other Heading: Reflections on Today's Europe*, Indiana University Press, 1992.

3 It seems that Kant's 1795 essay (*Zum ewigen Frieden. Ein philosophischer Entwurf*) has lost none of its relevance in today's discussions.

4 Cf. also Derrida, Jacques, *L'Autre cap*, Editions de Minuit, 1991.

Husserl's definition of Europe as an idea,[5] Derrida inquires both into the eidetic unity of Europe and how Europe itself is born from the idea of philosophy. While Husserl explains however that the teleological idea of Europe is undergoing a crisis in modernity as a result of sciences' naive desire for formal objectivism,[6] Derrida suggests there is no teleological reason for this crisis, and that the crisis itself does not reveal anything original. The idea of Europe is therefore intrinsically related to the idea of philosophy as an infinite task, which is why Derrida is not only a "European thinker", but a "thinker of Europe". What follows from such a position is therefore neither Eurocentrism nor anti-Eurocentrism, but rather a critical interrogation of European identity as the spiritual unity of Europe. Let us remind ourselves that the idea of Europe was born from the ancient idea and birth of philosophy, and later enriched by a multiplicity of sources and identities that intersect in European heritage. The other concept of Europe, as a "new figure", can be understood as having origins outside itself. Therefore, Europe is precisely this openness, or freedom, with regard to all dichotomous counter-positions (e.g. the Other). This is the true universality of Europe, not as a territory or a nation-state. The name "Europe" imposes itself as a concept and as a task of universality. As a consequence, Europe as the figure of the "passage" neither presupposes prior identity to be overcome, nor a new one to be achieved.[7] Rather, it is openness to otherness, transformation and permanent transition, and this is precisely why it has universal appeal. This is why Derrida used the French term "mondialisation" instead of the Anglo-American term "globalization".[8]

Derrida further asserts: "I believe that without Eurocentric illusions and pretensions, without the slightest European nationalism, without even much trust in Europe as it is or in the direction it is taking, we must fight for what this name represents today, of course, with the memory of the Enlightenment, but also with a guilty conscience for a responsible awareness of the totalitarian, genocidal and colonialist crimes of the past."[9] Jacques Derrida begins his compelling essay on contemporary

5 On this issue, cf. especially Gasché, Rodolphe, *Europe, Or The Infinite Task*, Stanford University Press, 2008, and Miettinen, Timo, *The Idea of Europe in Husserl's Phenomenology*, University of Helsinki, 2013.

6 Cf. very good overview in Alvis, Jason Wesley, "The Crisis of the Rogue: Husserl *under* Deconstruction", in *Paralog Journal*, January 2013.

7 Cf. Gasché, Rodolphe, *Europe, Or The Infinite Task*, *op. cit.*

8 Jacques Derrida extensively explains this problem in "What Does It Mean to Be a French Philosopher Today?" in *Paper Machine.* Stanford University Press, 2005, pp. 112-120.

9 Derrida, J., *The Other Heading*, *op. cit.*

world politics with the issue of European identity. He asks: *What is Europe?* How has Europe traditionally been defined and how is the current world situation changing that definition? Does the prospect of a New Europe demand not only a new definition of European identity but also a new way of thinking identity itself? If such Eurocentric biases are to be avoided, Derrida warns, the question of Europe must be asked in a new way; it must be asked by recalling *another heading*. Not only is it necessary for Europe to be responsible for the other, but its own identity is actually constituted by the other. Rejecting the easy solutions of Eurocentrism or anti-Eurocentrism, of total unification or complete dispersion, Derrida argues for the need to work from the Enlightenment values of liberal democracy while at the same time recalling that these values do not themselves ensure respect for the other. Referring to various texts of Marx, Husserl, and especially Valery, Derrida seeks to find a redefinition of European identity that includes respect both for difference and for universal values. *The Other Heading* appeals eloquently for a sustained effort at thinking through the complexity along with the multiple dangers and opportunities of the contemporary world situation without resorting to easy solutions. Here, Europe stands for a study of a *philosophical concept*. Derrida's argument for reinventing the idea of Europe (or European identity) focuses on the possibility that Europe be understood as "the beginning of a (his)story, the heading of which may always be changed". The "heading" Derrida speaks of is an idea of Europe as a heading, a *cape*, an appendix to the Asian body and a heading distinguishing that which is not Europe, which in its otherness is also constitutive of European identity. In other words, Derrida redefines European identity as a radical responsibility for itself, that is to say, Europeans must remind themselves of the heading of the other, "before which we must respond, and which we must *remember*, of which we must *remind ourselves*".[10] This need to remind oneself of the other is fundamental to the new Europe Derrida suggests, a Europe *beyond* Eurocentrism and anti-Eurocentrism.

Let us now turn to Habermas, who has been named "the last European", because of his mission to save the EU and his reluctance to see Europe consigned to the dustbin of world history. He clearly states: "I condemn the political parties. Our politicians have long been incapable of aspiring to anything whatsoever other than being re-elected. They have no political substance whatsoever, no convictions".[11] Therefore, I would like to refer to one of his articles published in the *Frankfurter Allgemeine*

10 Derrida, J., *op. cit.*

11 See interview in *Der Spiegel*, 47/2011.

Zeitung as well as in his book *Zur Verfassung Europas* (*On Europe's Constitution*),[12] which is basically a long essay in which he describes how the essence of our democracy has changed under pressure from the crisis and the frenzy of the markets. The addressees of his writings are EU politicians, accused of cynicism and of "turning their backs on the European ideals."[13] But does he have an answer to the question of which road democracy and capitalism should take? Habermas basically says that power has slipped from the hands of the people and shifted to bodies of questionable democratic legitimacy, such as the European Council. In essence, he believes that the technocrats have staged a quiet *coup d'état*. According to him, last year Angela Merkel and Nicolas Sarkozy (the couple known as "Merkozy") "agreed to a vague compromise (which is certainly open to interpretation) between German *economic liberalism* and French *etatism*, and all signs indicate that they would both like to transform the executive federalism enshrined in the Lisbon Treaty into intergovernmental supremacy of the European Council that runs contrary to the spirit of the agreement."[14] At this point Habermas refers to the system that Merkel and Sarkozy established during the crisis as a "post-democracy". The fact is that the European Parliament today barely has any influence.[15] The European Commission has "an odd, suspended position" without really being responsible for what it does. Most importantly, however, he points to the European Council, which was given a central role in the Lisbon Treaty. He sees the Council as a "governmental body that engages in politics without being authorized to do so". He also sees a Europe in which states are driven by the markets, in which the EU exerts massive influence over the formation of new governments (recently in Italy and Greece), and in which what he so passionately defends about Europe has been simply turned on its head. Of course, Habermas is a social philosopher who truly believes in the rationality of the people. He truly believes in the old (one might add: old-fashioned) ordered democracy, as well as in a public sphere that serves to make things better.

This is in a certain way a belief in the power of words and the rationality of discourse.[16] While at first glance it seems the activists of the Occupy

[12] cf. Suhrkamp edition in 2011, as well as Habermas, J., *The Crisis of the European Union: A Response*, Polity, *2012.*

[13] *Der Spiegel*, *op. cit.*

[14] *Der Spiegel*, *op. cit.*

[15] Many prominent authors also agree on this issue.

[16] Cf. obvious reference: his famous *The Theory of Communicative Action*, Beacon Press, 1985.

Wall Street movement refuse to formulate clear demands,[17] Habermas explained why he sees Europe as a project for civilization that must not be allowed to fail, and why the "global community" is not only feasible, but also necessary to reconcile democracy with capitalism. Otherwise, he thinks, we run the risk of a permanent "state of emergency" (let us recall here Carl Schmitt or Giorgio Agamben)[18] otherwise countries will simply be driven by the markets. For the first time in the history of the EU, we are actually experiencing a dismantling of democracy. There is an obvious lack of political union and of "embedded capitalism", a term Habermas uses to describe a market economy controlled by politics. As previously stated, decisions of the European Council, which infuse our everyday life, have essentially no legal or legitimate basis. The nation-state is still seen as a place in which the rights of citizens are best protected, and it is unclear how this notion could be implemented on a European level. The EU is not a commonwealth of states or a federation, but rather something new. Ultimately, it is an analysis of the failure of European politics. However, it seems that Habermas offers no way out, no concrete or tangible answer to the question of which road democracy and capitalism should take. Essentially, all he offers is the kind of vision that a constitutional theorist is capable of formulating. In the midst of the crisis, he still sees "the example of the European Union's elaborated concept of a constitutional cooperation between citizens and states" as the best way to build the "global community of citizens". The main conclusion is that Habermas is, after all, as some scholars have already properly pointed out, a *pragmatic optimist*. He does not say what steps will take us from worse off to better off; he says: "If the European project fails, then there is the question of how long it will take to reach the status quo again. Remember the German Revolution of 1848: When it failed, it took us (i.e. Germans) 100 years to regain the same level of democracy as before."[19]

Therefore, we are now in Europe's post-democratic era. The monopolisation of the EU by political elites risks reducing a sense of civic solidarity that is crucial to the European project. Only in this case are the EU citizens who elect and control the parliament in Strasbourg able to participate in a joint process of democratic will-formation reaching across national borders. "A dangerous asymmetry has developed because to date the European Union has been sustained and monopolised only by political elites – an asymmetry between the democratic participation of

17 See intriguing article by Slavoj Žižek: "Occupy Wall Street: what is to be done next?", in *Guardian*, 24 April 2012.

18 Especially in Schmitt's *The Concept of the Political* and Agamben's *Homo Sacer.*

19 This "warning" comes from his Paris lecture.

the peoples in what their governments obtain for them on the subjectively remote Brussels stage and the indifference, even apathy, of the citizens of the union regarding the decisions of their parliament in Strasbourg."[20] Such a regime makes it possible to transfer the imperatives of the market to national budgets without proper democratic legitimation. This would involve using the threat of sanctions and pressure on disempowered national parliaments to enforce non-transparent and informal agreements. Is there an alternative? If we read Habermas properly, the alternative is to "pursue the democratic legal domestication of the European Union further in a consistent way. Europe-wide civic solidarity cannot emerge if social inequalities between the member states become permanent structural features along the fault lines separating poor from rich nations."[21]

Let us now go back a decade, to the time when Derrida and Habermas together published an appeal/petition, an article that appeared simultaneously in two newspapers: in Germany in *Frankfurter Allgemeine Zeitung* as "After the War: The Rebirth of Europe", and in France in *Libération*, as "A Plea for a Common Foreign Policy".[22] This article, among other things, called for new European responsibilities "beyond all Eurocentrism" and the strengthening of international law and international institutions. Both Habermas and Derrida were explicitly working toward a new, constructed European identity, which must surely be some kind of world-view. In other words, only in a united "cosmopolis", in which the distinction between foreign and domestic politics is obsolete, could *Weltinnenpolitik* (a global interior policy) make any sense. Here is a quotation from the article: "An attractive – even infectious – 'vision' of a future Europe will not fall from heaven. Today such a vision can only be born of the unsettling experience of helplessness. But it can also result from the [inner] distress caused by the current situation, in which we Europeans are thrown back on ourselves. And it must be articulated in the wild cacophony of a public with many voices. If this topic has not to date made it on to the agenda, we intellectuals have failed."[23] The EU presents itself as a form of "governing beyond the national state", that could serve as an example of a post-national constellation. For a long time the European welfare state was also an example for others. At the level of the nation state, however, it has been forced into the defensive. But the level of social justice that the welfare state has attained should not be abandoned by a future policy aimed at taming capitalism. Why should Europe, having solved such enormous

---

[20] Cf. Habermas, J., "Europe's post-democratic era", in *Guardian*, 10 November 2011.

[21] *Ibid.*

[22] This joint declaration was issued on May 31, 2003.

[23] English translation of the respective article.

problems, shy away from the challenge of developing and defending a cosmopolitan order on the basis of international law?

Following that trail of the European welfare state and the lack of legitimacy of Eurocratic policies, Habermas tried, some years ago now, to answer the question "Why does Europe still need a constitution?" He stated:

> Europe is in the process of inventing a new political form, something more than a confederation but less than a federation – an association of sovereign states which pool their sovereignty only in very restricted areas to varying degrees, an association which does not seek to have the coercive power to act directly on individuals in the fashion of nation states. Therefore, the challenge before us is not to *invent* anything but to *conserve* the great democratic achievements of the European nation-state, beyond its own limits. These achievements include not only formal guarantees of civil rights, but levels of social welfare, education and leisure that are the precondition of both an effective private autonomy and of democratic citizenship.[24]

From this viewpoint, it is "clear that while the original political aims of European integration have lost much of their relevance, they have since been replaced by an even more ambitious political agenda."[25] Of course, rapid economic growth was the basis for a welfare state that provided the framework for the regeneration of post-war European societies. But the most important outcome of this regeneration has been the birth of ways of life that have allowed the wealth and national diversity of a multi-secular culture to become attractively renewed. The "European way of life" has become the content of a political project.

Here we are faced with a similar standpoint to Derrida, because Habermas urges us to consider a European project *beyond* the mere creation of monetary and economic union. He states: "today we need a broader perspective if Europe is not to decay into a mere market, sodden by globalization. For Europe is much more than a market. It stands for a model of society that has grown historically". He goes on:

> Economic globalization, whether we interpret it as no more than an intensification of long-range trends or as an abrupt shift towards a new transnational configuration of capitalism, shares with all processes of accelerated modernization some disquieting features. Eurosceptics reject a shift in the basis of legitimation of the Union from international treaties to a European constitution with the argument, that 'there are yet no European people'. This nation of citizens must not be confused with a community of fate, shaped by common descent, language and history. This confusion fails to capture the voluntaristic

24 Habermas, J., "Why Europe Needs a Constitution", in *New Left Review* 11, September-October 2011.

25 *Ibid.*

character of a civic nation, the collective identity of which exists neither independent of nor prior to the democratic process from which it springs. The artificial conditions in which national consciousness came into existence recall the empirical circumstances necessary for an extension of that process of identity formation beyond national boundaries. These are: the emergence of European civil society; the construction of a European-wide public sphere; and the shaping of a political culture that can be shared by all European citizens. At the same time, a European-wide public sphere needs to be embedded in a political culture shared by all. This widely perceived requirement has stimulated a troubled discourse among intellectuals, since it has been difficult to separate the question 'What is Europe?' from the fact that the achievements of European culture – which did not, in fact, seriously reflect upon its own nature and origin until the eighteenth or nineteenth centuries – have been diffused across the globe. What forms the common core of a European identity is the character of the painful learning process it has gone through, as much as its results.[26]

Taking it as a premise that a European Constitution is both feasible and desirable, let us one more time point out previously mentioned differences between the USA and the EU. According to Habermas's proposal, the European Union of nation-states would have to display the following general features:

1) Parliament that would resemble the Congress in *some* respects similar division of powers and, compared with the European parliamentary systems, relatively weak political parties;
2) The legislative 'chamber of nations' would have more competencies than the American Senate, and a Commission that would be much less powerful than the White House (thus splitting the classical functions of a strong Presidency between the two);
3) The European Court would be as influential as the Supreme Court for similar reasons (the regulatory complexity of an enlarged and socially diversified Union would require detailed interpretation of a principled constitution, cutting short the jungle of existing treaties).

Let us now go back to Derrida and try to elaborate his understanding of the differences between the European and American political projects. It seems that it is easier to answer the question "What is the USA?" than "What is Europe?". For Derrida, America is clearly Europe's Other. In other words, Derrida's notion is very much focused on the other and on difference. In contrast to Derrida's idea of America is, of course, Habermas's Europe: a Europe where identity predominates over

26 *Ibid.*

difference and where Kantian reason and the spirit of the Enlightenment have been unleashed to crush the darker passions that produced unspeakable destruction during World War Two.[27] Habermas's Europe is a transnational unity, a Europe of "constitutional patriotism". Moreover, he has in the past condemned Derrida's deconstructive approach as fostering a reversion to a pre-Enlightenment mystique as opposed to the project of modernity.

What is then the major difference between these two great thinkers? For Derrida (who was deconstructionist), in the joint petition mentioned above published ten years ago, the question was how can one mount a principled condemnation of terrorism if one has rejected or gone beyond enlightened reason and the value system associated with it? For the "Kantian modernist" Habermas, the question was how can Enlightenment reason still be considered relevant given that the era of modernism has seen totalitarianism and the Holocaust followed by global terrorism? Significantly, they both dealt with the relationship between terrorism and the Enlightenment, and though they embraced different views of it, they both placed themselves on the side of the Enlightenment. In that context, both Europe and America should be taken symbolically and metaphorically rather than literally. The ideal of cosmopolitanism as conceived by Derrida is derived from Kant and is thus firmly anchored in Enlightenment thought. Habermas' discourse ethics within a dialogical framework posits an ideal communicative setting within which all participants are oriented towards reaching a consensus and are given equal opportunity to present their claims. Only those claims that are universalizable from the standpoint of *all* perspectives are to command the consensus of all participants and hence to become morally binding on all. But, contrary to Derrida, Habermas considers the pathologies associated with the Enlightenment project as being external to it and external to modernity. Thus modernity and communicative ethics require the rational pursuit of freedom and equality for all.

Following the analysis I have tried to develop in this article, and combining different, though similar, notions of Europe, I will propose a conclusion. Europe is primarily a search for identity, a search for the "lost future". The main task today is therefore to build a cosmopolitan order that will guarantee perpetual peace in the world. Europe *is* and cannot be anything else but a *cosmopolitan project* embracing the transnational idea of freedom of the citizen and of humans in their identity. What is missing

27 Cf. Rosenfeld, Michel, "Derrida's Ethical Turn and America: Looking Back from the Crossroads of Global Terrorism and the Enlightenment", in *Cardozo Law Review*, 27: 2005.

today is in fact the subject of transnational politics as metapolitics of advent of freedom of "coming community" (Agamben). Only in this sense can Europe overcome neoliberal technocratic ideology and once again create itself as a project of new power beyond the limitations of nation-states, territorial sovereignty and the limited participation of European citizens in EU politics today.

The Declaration on the European Identity

The Claim for a "European Europe" in the Face of the World

Maria GĂINAR

There is no shadow of a doubt that the "Year of Europe" speech delivered on the 23rd of April, 1973 was a decisive factor standing at the origin of the Declaration on the European Identity. On that occasion Henry Kissinger, National Security Advisor to President Richard Nixon, put forward the idea that the Atlantic Partnership must be renewed in order to adapt to the international realities. The American initiative was a serious challenge for the nine partners of the European Political Cooperation (EPC)[1] who, with good reason, were rather hastily required to ask themselves whether this would bring about a "beatification" or a "strangulation".[2] Washington's proposal led the Nine towards a process that took them a bit by surprise: the need to define their place on the international arena, and therefore their identity facing the world.

By the end of June 1973, the idea of drafting a document on the European identity took shape across the Channel, receiving the support of the other partners a few weeks later. A great deal of work from the governing bodies of the EPC allowed for the successful completion of the process leading to the publication of the Declaration at the time of the Copenhagen Summit, on December 14th-15th. However, it became obvious ever since the fall of 1973, that the text being drafted was starting to

1 Launched in 1970, the European Political Cooperation was founded on consultation between the member states of the European Communities on foreign policy matters. Characterised by collaboration between Foreign Affairs ministries, it was based on a nucleus of regular meetings of the ministers of Foreign Affairs, of the Political Committee (made of political directors), of the European correspondents and of the national experts. CPE's main objective was to have Europe speak with one voice on the international arena. For further details on Political Cooperation, see Maria Găinar, *Aux origines de la diplomatie européenne: Les Neuf et la Coopération politique européenne de 1973 à 1980*, Bruxelles, Peter Lang, 2012, 642 p.

2 National Archives (NA), Paris, 5 AG 2/1023, Reykjavik meetings (May 31st-June 1st): "Second meeting between President Pompidou and President Nixon", May 31st, 1973.

build a life of its own, independent of the Euro-American relations topic. The question must be posed, then, whether the American initiative was, in fact, the mere catalyst of a process that was already ongoing and which, according to Étienne Davignon[3] was simply in tune with the times.[4]

1. Genesis of the Definition of the European Identity

If historic facts urge to point to the summer of 1973 as the origin of the Declaration on European Identity, awareness of this identity dates back to more distant times.[5] An overview of the past allows for a better understanding of the significance of the Declaration on European Identity and for underlining its genuine role, given that it has often been examined, even by its contemporaries, only through the Euro-American tensions.

A. Origins of the Process

The "European identity" syntagm entered the political vocabulary at the end of the 1960s and seems to have reached a climax at the beginning of the 1970s, with an increase in the number of speeches and writings on European identity. If before the 1960s, political officials "used to speak more willingly of Europe's personality", now they appeared to "increasingly prefer the term 'identity'".[6] A "willingness to explain Europe to the world"[7] comes about, writing itself in "the logic of a priority response to international reactions towards Europe".[8]

In the fall of 1970, Franco Maria Malfatti, President of the European Commission (July 1970-March 1972), draws attention to the fact that "awareness of what we already are and what we will become when [...] negotiations [on the United Kingdom's accession] will have been completed, is much more deeply rooted outside the Community than inside".[9] Convinced of Europe's increasing need to "fully express itself

3 Political director within the Belgian Ministry of Foreign Affairs between 1970 and 1976, Étienne Davignon chaired the Political Committee drafting the Luxembourg (1970) and Copenhagen (1973) Reports on Political Cooperation. He was a European Commissioner between 1977 and 1985 and passed the "Davignon plan" for the restructuring of European steel industry.

4 Interview with Étienne Davignon, March 6th, 2009.

5 Huber, Sophie, *Polyphonie sur l'identité européenne: Aux origines d'un discours identitaire 1962-1973*, thesis No. 811, defended at the University of Geneva in 2009, 371 p.

6 *Ibid.*, p. 236.

7 *Ibid.*, p. 214.

8 *Ibid.*, p. 241.

9 *Ibid.*, p. 211.

and its identity on the international arena",[10] President Malfatti declared in October 1971 that "it became increasingly urgent to look further and examine the effects of this structure on the international relations equilibrium".[11] Sicco Mansholt, President of the European Commission between April 1972 and January 1973, kept his speech on European identity in line with those of his predecessor. In July 1972, he declared before the European Parliament that "once created, the United Europe of the Ten will have to assert its personality".[12] While preparing the Paris Summit, in July 1972, Sicco Mansholt reiterated his ideas about the assertion of the European identity in a more pressing manner: "What are the tasks awaiting Europe? It must find its political identity – and it must do so during the conference at the Summit that is about to begin. On this occasion, Europe will have to clearly state its political objectives with regard to both the people of Europe and the rest of the world".[13]

If, by the end of the 1960s the European identity was a topic addressed in the interventions of European commissioners and deputies, at the beginning of the 1970s national leaders also take an interest in this subject. No major discontinuity can be detected between the EU players' discourse and that of political officials.[14] Thus, in March 1972 the French President Georges Pompidou declared, in the context of the European Communities' enlargement, that Great Britain's integration helps give the latter its true dimensions and possibilities and highlights Europe's identity in relation to the entire world".[15]

Two important factors trigger the acceleration of the process meant at defining European identity at the beginning of the 1970s. The first is the enlargement of the European Communities, now including new countries, among which a big one, the United Kingdom. The European Communities' enlargement from six to nine member states conferred them more weight and more visibility on the international arena, hence Europe's increasing need to define itself in relation to the world. The second factor refers to the increasing number of questions arising from non-member countries on the personality of Europe.[16] These interrogations coming from outside the EC fuel the discussion about a European identity, which progressively leads to the will to define Europe's role in the world.

---

[10] *Ibid.*, p. 236.
[11] *Ibid.*
[12] *Ibid.*, p. 212.
[13] *Ibid.*, p. 238.
[14] *Ibid.*, p. 241.
[15] *Ibid.*, p. 236.
[16] *Ibid.*, p. 210.

The convergence between the discourse of various officials at the beginning of the 1970s allows for a very important step towards coining a definition of the European identity during the conference of the Heads of State and Government held in Paris, on October 19th-20th, 1972. The final communiqué at the end of the conference seeks to draft a definition of the European identity in paragraphs 10 to 13, thus inaugurating a process that will lead, one year later, to the Declaration on the European Identity. The Heads of State and Government assert that "their efforts, deployed in order to build their Community, fail to reach their fuller meaning unless the member states manage to act together and face the increasing responsibilities incumbent upon Europe throughout the world".[17] At the same time, however, they restrict Europe's sphere of activity to the economic arena alone. Whereas on the one hand, they do not hesitate to envisage an increased development of their relations with developing, industrialised or Eastern Europe countries, on the other hand, they do not mention the political role that Europe will play on the international arena. Thus, "although focusing on spelling out Europe's political objectives" in relation to the world, the content of the paragraphs in relation to "foreign affairs" lacks precision.[18]

B. A Favourable Context against a Background of European-American Tensions

Following the Summit in Paris, the European identity topic returned to the forefront at the beginning of the summer of 1973. Three factors contributed to this comeback. The first is related to Euro-American relations, a topic already widely present in the discussions of the Nine – but with no common answer in sight. The stagnation of negotiations related to the Euro-American relations within the Political Cooperation progressively imposed the idea that it would be difficult, if not impossible, to present itself as a common front facing the United States, without having defined Europe's place in the world in the first place.[19]

The second factor was the American-Soviet agreement on nuclear war signed on June 22nd, 1973. The United States and the URSS committed to "prevent nuclear war, not only between them, but also between one of the two and a third country".[20] This event was considered by most

17 *La Coopération politique européenne (CPE)*, Office de presse et d'information du gouvernement fédéral, Bonn, 1982, pp. 40-42.

18 Huber, S., *Polyphonie sur l'identité européenne*, *op. cit.*, p. 239.

19 Archives of the French Ministry of Foreign Affairs (AMFA), Paris, 3792, Summary of Conclusions "VIIth Ministerial Meeting", June 28th, 1973.

20 Duroselle, Jean-Baptiste, *Histoire diplomatique de 1919 à nos jours*, Dalloz, Paris, 1993, p. 772.

European partners as compromising their security and their interests[21] and could only encourage the Nine to start defining their own identity facing the American-Soviet private agreement, which tended to impose itself since the SALT I was signed.[22]

Finally, the last factor resides in the Europeans' success during the multilateral negotiations preparing the Conference on Security and Cooperation in Europe – CSCE – (November 22nd, 1972-June 8th, 1973). Indeed, these negotiations represented a highly symbolical moment for the Nine, who asserted their identity facing the Soviet Union and more generally, facing the communist bloc.[23] Moreover, this success allowed them to fully understand their capacity to act and weigh in on the international chessboard, while also granting them the confidence they needed to rapidly engage in the process of asserting their European identity.

2. "1973" and the Drafting of the Declaration on the European Identity

It is in this favourable frame of mind that the United Kingdom decided, at the end of June 1973, to propose to its partners the elaboration of a document on the European identity.[24] No more than five months passed between the British initiative and the document being drawn up. The Nine came to a speedy agreement, indeed.

A. Three Projects, as Many Visions

At the end of the summer of 1973, several national documents (British, Irish and French) were registered with the Danish Presidency, which had asked the member states for their contributions to fuel the discussions.[25]

---

21 AMFA, Paris, 3795, c/o "Political Committee of the Nine (Helsinki, July 5th-6th): Soviet-American agreement on the prevention of nuclear wars", July 10th, 1973; AMFA, Paris, 3792, c/o "Conversation with M. Ducci: European Political Cooperation", July 11th, 1973.

22 Melandri, Pierre, "Une relation très spéciale: La France, les États-Unis et l'année de l'Europe, 1973-1974" in *Georges Pompidou et l'Europe*, Complexes, Bruxelles, 1995, p. 114.

23 Historic Archives of the European Union (HAEU), Florence, EN 73, "A policy of the Community in relation to the countries of Eastern Europe", April 11th, 1972; HAEU, Florence, EN 1869, "Speech by Michel Jobert at the United Nations", October 10th, 1973.

24 Möckli, Daniel, *European Foreign Policy during the Cold War: Heath, Brandt, Pompidou and the Dream of Political Unity*, I.B. Tauris, London-New York, 2009, pp. 161-162.

25 Documents on British Policy Overseas (DPBO), *The Year of Europe: America, Europe and the Energy Crisis, 1972-1974* (CD-ROM), 3rd series, Vol. IV, 2005, document

The three texts stood out by virtue of their highly different approaches to the European identity concept.

The British document, delivered to the EPC in mid-August, follows the line adopted by London at the beginning of summer. While being the most substantial of the projects from afar, the text prepared by the Foreign Office[26] is rather an analysis whose force of proposal is rather shaky. Focusing almost exclusively on Euro-American relations, it stresses the upcoming discussions with Washington and advocates the Nine's need to define their identity in relation to the United States. The latter idea is justified by the fact that Europe would have a hard time imposing itself on the international arena without having reached common grounds in relation to Washington beforehand. According to the British text, coining a definition of the European identity would have to allow the Nine, on the one hand, to immediately respond to the American initiative on the "Year of Europe" and on the other, to face outside economic, financial, political or military pressure arising from China, Japan, the Soviet Union or the United States in the years to come.[27]

The Irish document embraces a new perspective, favouring a conceptual approach. It defines the identity of the Nine, while referring to the institutional identity expressed in the treaties, to the results obtained within the EPC and to the aspiration towards a European Union mentioned in the communiqué of the Paris conference. Moreover, the authors of the text recommend that the Nine maintain the current scope of their identity during possible conversations with Richard Nixon, avoiding to take up subjects that had not been the object of detailed discussion among themselves. Lastly, the Irish description of the European identity underlines the primacy of internal factors over external ones and rules out any aspiration to become a superpower on Europe's part.[28]

Based upon a draft prepared at the end of July by the Western Europe Division[29] of the *Quai d'Orsay*,[30] the French document is more synthetic

213, tel 1770 in Copenhagen, "Transatlantic Relations", August 31st, 1973, document 191, tel 188 in Copenhagen, "Europe/United States Relations", August 8th, 1973.

26 By metonymy, the Foreign Office refers to the British Ministry of Foreign Affairs.

27 AMFA, Paris, 3792, British project: "The Identity of the Nine Vis A Vis the United States", undated (most probably, this is a document elaborated at the end of July, beginning of August, 1973).

28 AMFA, Paris, 3792, Irish project on the European identity, undated (most probably, this is a document elaborated at the end of July, beginning of August, 1973).

29 AMFA, Paris, 3810, c/o "Ministerial meeting (Copenhagen, July 23rd): Europe/United States relations: Possible content of a document to be drafted on the European identity in relation to the United States", July 20th, 1973.

30 By metonymy, the *Quai d'Orsay* refers to the French Ministry of Foreign Affairs.

and general than the other two texts. Made of two parts, it strives to define the European identity starting from the common heritage, interests and obligations of the Nine, as well as their level of cohesion towards the rest of the world. Among the constitutive elements of the European identity, the document quotes: the common heritage of a common civilisation, the interests and characteristics ensuing from history and from natural and economic conditions, the implications of the concentration of powers and responsibilities in the hands of a very small number of major powers, Europe's need to equip itself with appropriate defence means, as well as the openness of the European construction to other European nations sharing the same ideals.

By dealing with the European identity in relation to the rest of the world, the French document underlines the will of the Nine to play an active, dynamic role in international politics and to define common grounds. Then follows a presentation of the states or of the groups of countries with which the Nine would like to have strong relations: developing countries, especially in Africa and around the Mediterranean, the United States, Japan, Canada, Eastern countries and China. By way of conclusion, the French project stresses the fact that the Nine will take part in the next international negotiations with an open mind, but making sure that neither the constitutive elements of their unity, nor the fundamental objectives of their internal evolution are questioned.[31]

The French document is undoubtedly the one that changed the order of things once and for all in the beginning of September 1973. While the British and Irish projects inscribe the European identity matter within the problematics of the Euro-American relations, the text drafted by the *Quai d'Orsay* increases the range of the debate through a global, ambitious approach. Furthermore, the French project is the only one to avoid the trap of an analytical discourse and to take on European identity under the covering of a believable sketch. It is therefore not surprising that it was quick to obtain the support of the nine partners and be considered a starting point for the drawing up of a document on the European identity.[32]

B. The Negotiations around the Text

The turning point of the process of defining the European identity occurs during the reunion of the Political Committee held on September

31 AMFA, Paris, 3792, French project: "About the European identity", September 4th, 1973.

32 AMFA, Paris, 3795, "Reunion of the Political Committee (September 4th-5th): Europe/United States relations", September 5th, 1973; *The Year of Europe*, *op. cit.*, document 213, Copenhagen tel 219, "Transatlantic relations", September 5th, 1973.

4th-5th, 1973. Following a round of discussions, the political directors agree that the writing process "should not be dictated, either in its sketching or in its schedule, by any possible short-term considerations".[33] They put the Presidency in charge of preparing, with the ministers' meeting in mind, "a text pointing out the fundamental elements of the European identity"[34] based chiefly on the French document.

A week later, the ministers' discussions proceed on the basis of the report drawn up by the Danish Presidency. The document identifies three principles on which the identity of the Nine should be founded: internal cohesion within the Community, the positions and responsibilities of the Nine in relation to the rest of the world and the dynamic character of the European construction. Next comes a more detailed presentation of their content emphasising the common values and heritage of the Nine, their attachment to the construction of Europe and the establishment of common grounds, their determination to pin down Europe's position in international affairs and to adapt the definition of their identity to subsequent evolutions.[35] As revealed throughout the discussions, the ministers were quick to agree that the works on the European identity should be based on the orientations defined in the document drafted by the Presidency and on the French contribution.[36]

The process of writing the document was then brought over to the European correspondents' group. It went forth without major difficulties. There were only a few slightly problematic points, which made differences in opinions arise. The German representative strived to tone down the paragraphs that could present Europe as a new power appearing to have the ambition to become a superpower. His objective was in fact to avoid offending Washington, especially given the tense context of the fall of 1973. The British delegate wished for a reference to be made to the Nine's will to progressively define a "common foreign policy".[37] Finally, facing the scepticism showed by the French, he was convinced to give up. Paris spoke against that formula, considering that such a policy risked

---

33 AMFA, Paris, 3792, "Report of the President of the Political Committee on the deliberations of the Committee on the European identity", September 7th, 1973.

34 AMFA, Paris, 3795, c/o "Reunion of the Political Committee (September 4th-5th): Europe/United States relations", September 5th, 1973.

35 AMFA, Paris, 3792, "Report of the President of the Political Committee on the deliberations of the Committee on the European identity", September 7th, 1973.

36 AMFA, Paris, 3810, c/o "Ministerial meeting on Political Cooperation (Copenhagen, September 10th-11th): European identity", September 12th, 1973.

37 AMFA, Paris, 3795, Note "Political Committee of November 12th-13th": European identity, November 8th, 1973.

being Atlantist.[38] The French correspondent tried in vain to convince his counterparts to include the triptych "détente, entente, cooperation" in the paragraph concerning Eastern Europe. Not wanting to go beyond the boundaries set by the Paris Summit communiqué, which included only the words "détente" and "cooperation", the other delegates convinced him to finally give up the "entente" concept.[39]

The European identity project finds its way on the ministers' discussion table on November 20th, 1973. An agreement is quickly reached on the text elaborated by the correspondents, including on the paragraph related to defence. In fact, following a brief exchange, the Irish minister, Garret FitzGerald, agrees to leave all reservations behind, not wanting to oppose the consensus reached by his eight partners.[40] Thus, the very last obstacle standing against the adoption of this document was dismissed. However, due do the British minister Alec Douglas-Home's insistence, the Nine agreed to ask the Political Committee to put the finishing touches on the paragraph concerning the relations with the United States, so as to "put a smile on it".[41] The Euro-American tensions during the October War are far from being irrelevant to the sensitivity manifested by the British leader about this.

3. Contents and Impact of the Declaration

The Nine published the declaration on the European identity on the second day of the Copenhagen Summit, on December 15th, 1973. They justified their approach at the very beginning of the text, stating that drawing up a document on the European identity allowed them to better define "their relations with other countries and their responsibilities and the place which they occupy in world affairs". Furthermore, they underlined the fact that they had defined this identity in a dynamic perspective and with the intention of scrutinizing it further in the light of the progress made in what the construction of Europe is concerned.[42]

The declaration, a genuine foreign policy project, is made of three parts. First of all, it emphasises the Nine's internal cohesion while

38 AMFA, Paris, 3795, Note "Political Committee of November 12th-13th", November 9th, 1973.

39 AMFA, Paris, 3795, Note "Political Committee of November 12th-13th: European Identity", November 8th, 1973.

40 AMFA, Paris, 3810, c/o "Ministerial meeting on Political Cooperation (Copenhagen, November 20th)", November 22nd, 1973.

41 AMFA, Paris, 3810, c/o "Ministerial meeting on Political Cooperation (Copenhagen, November 20th)", November 22nd, 1973.

42 *Europe, Documents*, No. 779, December 15th, 1973.

underlining the values on which the European partners' policy is based. Thus, the Nine identify several key elements of the European identity: "respect for legal, political and moral values", the preservation of "the rich variety of their national cultures", the fact that they share "the same perception of life, based on the desire to create a society conceived and built to the service of mankind", the defence of "the principles of the representative democracy, of the rule of law, of social justice – the purpose of the economic progress – and of the respect for human rights". Another aspect of the European identity highlighted by the Nine refers to their desire to successfully complete the construction of Europe by applying the provisions of the Treaties of Paris and Rome and those of the Luxembourg and Copenhagen Reports having in mind to "transform, before the end of the decade, the totality of their relations into a European Union". Moreover, they believe that "such a variety of cultures within the framework of the same civilisation [...], the fact that they share the same values and principles, [the same] outlook on life [...] give European identity its original character and its distinctive dynamism". Finally, the Nine declare the construction of Europe "open to other European nations sharing the same ideals and the same objectives".[43]

The last paragraphs of this part are dedicated to the place of the Nine – seen as an entity – in the world. What is then emphasised is the importance "of very tight bonds" formed "with many parties in the world [that] represent a genuine guarantee of international progress and balance" and on "the positive influence" that they can exert "upon economic relations throughout the world, having in mind the improvement of the well-being of all". Moreover, they emphasise that "international problems can hardly be solved by each of them alone" and that "the changes that occurred in the world and the increasing concentration of power and responsibilities in the hands of a very restricted number or great powers imply that Europe must unite and [...] speak with one voice if it wants to make itself heard and to play the international part it should play". Finally, the Nine assert that in order to reach their crucial objective, namely peace preservation, they have to work on their own security. Thus, "those who are members of the Atlantic Alliance believe that at the present moment, there is no real alternative to the security insured by the US nuclear weapons and the presence of North American armed forces in Europe and agree that with regard to its relative military vulnerability, and if it wants to preserve its independence, Europe must keep its commitments and make sure that it can count on an adequate defence".[44]

---

43 *Ibid.*

44 *Europe, Documents*, No. 779, December 15th, 1973.

The second part of the declaration is dedicated to the definition of the European identity in relation to the world. Being a new player on the international scene, the Nine declared from the very beginning that European unification is "not directed against anyone in particular, nor is it inspired by a will of power of any kind" but, quite on the contrary, it is meant to be an element of balance and to prompt cooperation with all nations, whatever their dimension, culture or social system". And "this desire must progressively lead the Nine towards defining common grounds in what foreign policy is concerned". Determined to play an active role in world affairs while abiding by the objectives and principles of the United Nations Charter, the Nine assert their willingness to progressively elaborate a common policy towards non-member countries. This policy will have to rest upon three principles: the relations with non-member countries "must not compromise, delay or affect the [Nine's] wish to make progress towards [...] the European Union"; "during future negotiations [...] the chosen frameworks and procedures will have to allow for the European entity's specific character to be respected"; "in their bilateral contacts [...] the Community's member countries will increasingly rely on common positions established among themselves".[45]

Then follows a programmatic presentation of the policy the Nine intend to carry on throughout the world, presenting the objectives they want to pursue in their relations with non-member countries: strengthen the relations with the other countries in the Council of Europe, associated countries and the countries around the Mediterranean basin; cooperate in the development of African countries; participate in the establishment and preservation of peace, stability and progress in the Middle-East region; achieve a constructive dialogue with the United States, Japan, Canada and the other industrialised countries; pursue a policy of détente and cooperation with the Soviet Union and Eastern Europe countries; build up relations with China, other Asian and Latin American countries.[46]

Numerous authors have pondered upon the order in which the above countries are enumerated in this part of the declaration. The hypotheses they have put forward are many: "a conscious effort from Europeans to organise their partnerships in distinct and sometimes conflicting groups" (Yves Delayahe); "a complex endeavour aiming at classifying the various world players around [Europe] that leads to a genuine imaginary reconstruction of the world order" broken into "concentric circles corresponding to various economic and political proximity degrees" (Anne Le Naëlou); "a hierarchy" that places "strengthening ties with European countries well

45 *Ibid.*

46 *Europe*, *Documents*, No. 779, December 15th, 1973.

before the revision of the Transatlantic relation and relegates Asia and Latin America to the end of the pack" (Luisa Passerini); "a map of Europe's international relations network" (Sophie Huber).[47] If opinions seem to be quite divided in what this enumeration is concerned, they rather seem to converge so as to the main objective pursued by the Nine: the assertion of "Europe's new stature as an international power striving to synthesize all dialogues" carried out since 1960s with the rest of the world.[48]

Finally, in the third part, taking into consideration the dynamic character of the construction of Europe, the Nine conclude by stating that they will do their utmost to "progressively define their identity in relation to the other political entities". Thus, they are aware of "strengthening their internal cohesion and contributing to the elaboration of a European policy *stricto sensu*" that will facilitate the transformation of their relations into a European Union.[49] This last chapter, clearly shorter than the other two, is by no means insignificant. It reflects the spirit in which the declaration was written, namely the Nine's strong ambition, determination and confidence. Encouraged in their convictions by the successes achieved during the year 1973 at the CSCE, in the Middle East and facing the United States, the Europeans seem to be determined to place Europe once again at the very core of the international relations network and to strengthen its role by intensifying the European process.

The political will showing through the declaration on the European identity is in strong contrast with the reactions triggered by its publication. Its heterogeneous impact is largely explained by the troubled context in which the Copenhagen Summit took place. In the Communities' member states, the press seemed to be more preoccupied with the Nine's discussions on energy matters, regional funds or the principle of periodical summit meetings.[50] As for the reactions of non-member countries, they vary according to their interest in the matter. In Europe, the Swiss and Austrian press overlook the subject. If, in Norway and Spain, journalists make references to the declaration on the European identity, they do so either to underline the still crude unity of the Nine, judging by their inability to agree on energy-related issues, or to draw attention upon the isolation risk that might entail the Nine's future progress regarding cohesion. In the Arab world, journals are largely unaware of the publication of the declaration and choose to emphasise above all the discussions

47 See Huber, S., *Polyphonie sur l'identité européenne*, *op. cit.*, pp. 306-307.

48 *Ibid.*, p. 307.

49 *Europe*, *Documents*, No. 779, December 15th, 1973.

50 AMFA, Paris, 3789, c/o "Following the Copenhagen meeting: The reaction of the press in our partners' countries", December 28th, 1973.

taking place outside the Summit, between the Nine and Arab ministers.[51] China's viewpoint is made public via the *New China News Agency*. Highly parsimonious in its assessments, this agency simply states that the Copenhagen Summit "proved the Europeans' will to increase their political cooperation, to define their 'identity' and to accelerate their progress towards the European Union". The reactions of Eastern European countries and more specifically of the USSR stand out as they broadly reject the declarations resulting from the Summit. Because of its "political-military integration", "Little Europe" is accused of being against the "détente that has been embracing the entire continent". In the United States, the press remains silent, by and large. The *New York Times* is the only one to focus on the declaration, publishing its full text. However, the comments it sparks off are highly negative. The author of the article states that "the document shows that the Nine are setting off in the opposite direction to that of the special relations" proposed by Henry Kissinger and that it "clearly reflects the French viewpoint on Europe's independence, the equal rights and sovereignty of its member states".[52]

The few comments made about the declaration on the European identity reveal sceptical, even hostile attitudes. Two levels of analysis ensue from these reactions. The first shows that there is a gap between the image that Europeans would like to present to the world and the image that is reflected back to them. The second, which is representative of the American and Soviet' attitude, proves that the Nine's desire to carry out a twofold statement facing the United States and the Soviet Union did not go unnoticed. And these negative reactions, predictable to a certain extent, reveal the fact that the Europeans have reached their objective, at least on a symbolic, declaratory level.

*

* *

It is clear that the Declaration on the European identity embodies solidarity and unity, which were cultivated by Europeans particularly throughout 1973, and therefore it represents the birth act of the Nine as a distinct entity on the international arena. However, since it is a result of the convergence of a certain number of external factors, especially pressure from the Americans, the Nine's cohesion is still fragile and will soon be put to the test by the combined effects of the October War and Henry Kissinger's determination not to give in to the common front of the Nine.

---

51 AMFA, Paris, 3789, c/o "The Copenhagen Summit of the Nine: Reactions of non-member countries", December 28th, 1973.

52 AMFA, Paris, 3789, c/o "Reactions of the American press to the Copenhagen Summit", December 17th, 1973.

The Authors

Violeta Beširević is a Professor of Law at Union University Law School Belgrade, Serbia. Her recent works include *Public Law in Serbia: Twenty Years After*, ed. (London, European Public Law Organization & Esperia Publications Ltd, 2012); "A Short Guide To Militant Democracy: Some Remarks on the Strasbourg Jurisprudence", in *European Yearbook of Human Rights 2012*, eds. Wolfgang Benedek *et al.*, Antwerp, Intersentia, Wien, NW Verlag, 2012, pp. 243-258. She also authored the book *Euthanasia: Legal Principles and Policy Choices*, Florence, European Press Academic Publishing, 2006.

Patrice Canivez, Professor of Moral and Political Philosophy at the University of Lille, is Chair of the Institute Eric Weil and member of the research group UMR 8163 "Savoirs, Textes, Langage". His most significant works include: *Eduquer le citoyen?*, Paris, Hatier, 1995 (2nd ed.); *Weil*, Paris, Les Belles Lettres, 2004 (2nd ed.); *Qu'est-ce que la nation?*, Paris, Vrin, 2004; *L'Ethique et le soi chez Paul Ricoeur* (P. Canivez et L. Couloubaritsis eds.), V. d'Ascq, Presses Universitaires du Septentrion, 2013. Recent publications include: "Pathologies of Recognition", in *Philosophy and Social Criticism*, October 2011, 37: 851-887; "Paul Ricoeur et l'éthique aristotélicienne" in *L'Ethique et le soi chez Paul Ricoeur*, *op. cit.*

Nenad Dimitrijević is Professor in the Department of Political Science of Central European University in Budapest, Hungary. Selected works: *Duty to Respond. Mass Crime, Denial, and Collective Responsibility* (Budapest, CEU Press, 2011); five entries in *Encyclopedia of Transitional Justice* (Cambridge, Cambridge University Press, 2012); "Moral Knowledge and Mass Crime: A Critical Reading of Moral Relativism", in *Philosophy and Social Criticism*, Vol. 36, No. 2, 2010.

Alexandre Dupeyrix is Associate Professor at the University Paris-Sorbonne (Department of German Studies). His field of research concerns political philosophy and German history of ideas. Among his publications: *Comprendre Habermas* (Paris, Armand Colin, 2009); *Le pacifisme allemand du Reich wilhelmien à la fin de la République de Weimar 1890-1933* (ed.), *Cahiers IRICE*, No. 8, juillet 2011; *Habermas. Citoyenneté et responsabilité* (Paris, Maison des Sciences de l'Homme, 2012).

Maria Găinar graduated from the College of Europe in Bruges and obtained her PhD in Contemporary History in 2011. She is a member of the research group "Frontières, acteurs et représentations de l'Europe

(FARE)" of the University of Strasbourg. Most recent publication: *Aux origines de la diplomatie européenne: Les Neuf et la Coopération politique européenne de 1973 à 1980*, Bruxelles, 2012 (awarded the Jean-Baptiste Duroselle Prize 2012).

Tanasije Marinković is Assistant Professor of Constitutional Law at the Faculty of Law, University of Belgrade. He received his PhD degree from the Faculty of Law, University of Belgrade (2009). He also studied and researched at the University of Oxford, Institute of Federalism in Fribourg, Institute of Human Rights in Strasbourg, and Central European University in Budapest. For more than ten years now he has been the Secretary General of the Serbian Association of Constitutional Law. He has published extensively on constitutional law and human rights law topics, primarily in Serbian, but also in English and French, including the *Electoral Systems of the European Union Member States* and *Dictionary of Liberal Democracy* (co-authorship).

Gérard Raulet is Professor of the History of Ideas at the University Paris-Sorbonne and Chair of the Weimar Culture Research Group at the Foundation Maison des Sciences de l'Homme. Main publications in the last years: *Critical Cosmology. Essays on Nations and Globalization*, Lanham MD, Lexington Books 2005; *Das Zwischenreich der symbolischen Formen. Ernst Cassirers Erkenntnistheorie, Ethik und Politik im Spannungsfeld von Historismus und Neukantianismus*, Frankfurt/M. & al., Peter Lang 2005; *La philosophie allemande depuis 1945*, Paris, Armand Colin 2006; *Republikanische Legitimität und politische Philosophie heute*, Münster, Westfälisches Dampfboot 2012; Critical edition: Walter BENJAMIN, *Werke und Nachlaß. Kritische Gesamtausgabe*, t. XIX: Über den Begriff der Geschichte, Frankfurt/M., Suhrkamp 2010.

Tonči Valentić is a freelance researcher, lecturer and translator, based in Zagreb, Croatia. He obtained his B.A. in Philosophy and Literature in Zagreb, M.A. in Sociology and Anthropology in Budapest, and is currently finishing his PhD dissertation in Sociology in Ljubljana. His publications include: *Multiple Modernities: From Anthropology to Pornography* (2006), Essays on Ontology of Photography (2013) and Archipelago of Contemporary Philosophy (forthcoming September 2014).

Dragica Vujadinović is a Full Professor at the Faculty of Law, University of Belgrade and teaches Political and Legal Theory. Her publications include: *Političke i pravne teorije* (*Political and Legal Theories*, Beograd 1996); *Politička filozofija Ronalda Dvorkina* (*The Political Philosophy of Ronald Dworkin*, Beograd, 2007); *Civilno društvo i političke institucije* (*Civil Society and Political Institutions*, Beograd, 2009); *Civil Society in Contemporary Context*, Belgrade 2009; *Democracy and Human Rights in the EU* (co-authored with M. Jovanović and R. Etinski), Maribor/Belgrade 2009; *Serbia in the Maelstrom of Political Changes*, Belgrade 2009.

EUROCLIO – Published Books

N° 81 – *The European Community and the World. A Historical Perspective*. Giuliana Laschi (ed.), 2014.

N° 80 – *Christian Democrat Internationalism. Its Action in Europe and Worldwide from Post World War II until the 1990s. Volume II: The Development (1945-1979). The Role of Parties, Movements, People*. Jean-Dominique Durand (ed.), 2013.

N° 79 – *Christian Democrat Internationalism. Its Action in Europe and Worldwide from Post World War II until the 1990s. Volume I: The Origins*. Jean-Dominique Durand (ed.), 2013.

N° 78 – *Investment Banking History. National and Comparative Issues (19th-21st centuries)*. Hubert Bonin & Carlo Brambilla (eds.), 2013.

N° 77 – *Citizenship and Solidarity in the European Union. From the Charter of Fundamental Rights to the Crisis, the State of the Art*. Mariana Canotilho, Pedro Madeira Froufe & Alessandra Silveira (eds.), 2013.

N° 76– *The OSCE: Soft Security for a Hard World. Competing Theories for Understanding the OSCE*. Roberto Dominguez (ed.), 2013.

N° 75– *Euroscepticism, Europhobia and Eurocriticism. The Radical Parties of the Right and Left* vis-à-vis *the European Union*. Cesáreo Rodríguez-Aguilera de Prat, 2013.

N° 74 – *Fermer les mines en construisant l'Europe. Une histoire sociale de l'intégration européenne*. Nicolas Verschueren, 2012

N° 73 – *Reflets de la construction européenne. Réflexions, références et refus du débat sur l'Europe*. Bertrand Vayssière (dir.), 2012.

N° 72 – *The International Relations of Local Authorities. From Institutional Twinning to the Committee of the Regions: Fifty Years of European Integration History*. Fabio Zucca, 2012.

N° 71 – *Histoire du Conseil de l'Europe (1949-2009)*. Birte Wassenberg, 2012.

N° 70 – *The EU, Security and Transatlantic Relations*. Finn Laursen (ed.), 2012.

N° 69 – *Européanisation au XX*e *siècle. Un regard historique / Europeanisation in the 20*th *Century. The Historical Lens*. Matthieu Osmont, Émilia Robin-Hivert, Katja Seidel, Mark Spoerer & Christian Wenkel (dir./eds.), 2012.

N° 68 – *Consensus and European Integration. An Historical Perspective / Consensus et intégration européenne. Une perspective historique*. Daniela Preda & Daniele Pasquinucci (eds./dir.), 2012.

N° 67 – *Générations de fédéralistes européens depuis le XIX*e *siècle. Individus, groupes, espaces et réseaux*. Geneviève Duchenne et Michel Dumoulin (dir.), 2012.

N° 66 – *Raymond Aron, penseur de l'Europe et de la nation.* Giulio De Ligio (dir.), 2012.

N° 65 – *Europe Twenty Years after the End of the Cold War. The New Europe, New Europes? / L'Europe vingt ans après la fin de la guerre froide. Nouvelle Europe, nouvelles Europes?* Bruno Arcidiacono, Katrin Milzow, Axel Marion & Pierre-Étienne Bourneuf (eds./dir.), 2012.

N° 64 – *Aux origines de la diplomatie européenne. Les Neuf et la Coopération politique européenne de 1973 à 1980.* Maria Gainar, 2012.

N° 63 – *Europe and the Middle East. The hour of the East?* Birte Wassenberg & Giovanni Faleg (eds.), 2012.

N° 62 – *Quelle architecture pour un code européen de droit international privé ?* Marc Fallon, Paul Lagarde, Sylvaine Poillot-Peruzzetto (dir.), 2011.

N° 61 – *La construction d'un espace euro-méditerranéen. Genèses, mythes et perspectives.* Houda Ben Hamouda et Mathieu Bouchard (dir.), 2012.

N° 60 – *Innovations et transferts de technologie en Europe du Nord-Ouest aux XIXe et XXe siècles.* Jean-François Eck et Pierre Tilly (dir.), 2011.

N° 59 – *Novel Outlooks on the Marshall Plan. American Aid and European Re-Industrialization.* Fransceca Fauri & Paolo Tedeschi (eds.), 2011.

N° 58 – *Europe in the International Arena during the 1970s. Entering a Different World / L'Europe sur la scène internationale dans les années 1970. À la découverte d'un nouveau monde.* Antonio Varsori & Guia Migani (eds./dir.), 2011.

N° 57 – *Cultures nationales et identité communautaire. Un défi pour l'Europe ? / National Cultures and Common Identity. A Challenge for Europe?* Marloes Beers & Jenny Raflik (dir./eds.), 2010.

N° 56 – *Les trajectoires de l'innovation technologique et la construction européenne. Des voies de structuration durable ? / Trends in Technological Innovation and the European Construction. The Emerging of Enduring Dynamics?* Christophe Bouneau, David Burigana & Antonio Varsori (dir./eds.), 2010.

N° 55 – *L'OTAN et l'Europe. Quels liens pour la sécurité et la défense européenne ?* Birte Wassenberg, Giovanni Faleg et Martin W. Mlodecki (dir.), 2010.

N° 54 – *The Road Europe Travelled Along.* Daniele Pasquinucci and Daniela Preda (eds.), 2010.

N° 53 – *Vivre et construire l'Europe à l'échelle territoriale de 1945 à nos jours.* Yves Denéchère et Marie-Bénédicte Vincent (dir.), 2010.

Euroclio European Network

together with the SEGEI Network

Coordination : Chaire Jean Monnet d'histoire
de l'Europe contemporaine (Cehec)
Collège Erasme, 1, place Blaise-Pascal, B-1348 Louvain-la-Neuve

Germany

Jürgen Elvert
Wilfried Loth

Belgium

Julie Cailleau
Jocelyne Collonval
Yves Conrad
Gaëlle Courtois
Pascal Deloge
Geneviève Duchenne
Vincent Dujardin
Michel Dumoulin
Roch Hannecart
Pierre-Yves Plasman
Béatrice Roeh
Corine Schröder
Caroline Suzor
Pierre Tilly
Arthe Van Laer
Jérôme Wilson
Natacha Wittorski

Spain

Enrique Moradiellos
Mercedes Samaniego Boneu

France

Françoise Berger
Marie-Thérèse Bitsch
Gérard Bossuat
Éric Bussière
Jean-François Eck
Catherine Horel
Philippe Mioche
Marine Moguen-Toursel
Sylvain Schirmann
Matthieu Trouvé
Laurent Warlouzet
Emilie Willaert

Hungary

Gergely Fejérdy

Italy

David Burigana
Elena Calandri
Eleonora Guasconi
Luciano Segreto
Antonio Varsori

Luxemburg

Charles Barthel
Etienne Deschamps
Jean-Marie Kreins
René Leboutte
Robert Philippart
Corine Schröder
Gilbert Trausch

The Netherlands

Anjo Harryvan
Jan W. Brouwer
Jan van der Herst

Poland

Józef Laptos
Zdzisiaw Mach

Switzerland

Antoine Fleury
Lubor Jilek